The Mad Hatter

The Role of Mercury in the Life of Lewis Carroll

For My Sister

I had a sad dream that you were sleeping.

It seemed so real.

Table of Contents

The Mad Hatter

The King of the people's hearts was lost in a sort of *dream*. It had begun as a growing difficulty with the royal legs but reached a crisis with a violent spasmodic attack of the stomach. The disorder continued with more or less violence through a range of different physical symptoms until the medicines the doctors were forced to use to save the King's life *repelled* the disorder *upon the brain* with *an agitation and flurry of spirits, which gave him hardly any rest.* Finally, outright delirium overtook him, *direct lunacy.* One of the first medicines the lunacy doctors proposed was the mercurial compound, calomel, but it did little to benefit the *main complaint.* The Speaker of the House of Commons was concerned about changes to the government proposed by the Prime Minister during the King's illness. *Suppose him to awake out of the sort of dream, in which he now is?* How would he react? A nervous Parliament spent months debating the technicalities of a Regency Bill which would give the power of the executive authority to the King's eldest son, and it had just passed in the House of Commons when the King *did* awake. When he did, he was not angered over the measures which his court had taken to try to compensate for his illness, but he did send the lunacy doctors away. It *had* all seemed *like a dream*, but he remembered enough of what had passed to never want to set eyes on Willis and his sons ever again.

Part I

The Beginning—His Father's World.

Charles Dodgson the Senior

Clouded mind and sluggish will,--All my life is full of ill! Give me, give me—one blue pill. A ten-mile walk is better still.

-William Allingham

The purpose of this book is to examine the role of mercury in the life of Lewis Carroll, the author of the renowned *Alice's Adventures in Wonderland*, and the creator of the Mad Hatter, an iconic character whose name has become synonymous with mercury poisoning. Many people have asked whether the Mad Hatter suffered from mercury poisoning, but the more important question, perhaps, is whether Lewis Carroll himself suffered from mercury poisoning. He was, without question, exposed to mercury in the course of his photography, and he very likely experienced further exposure due to the extraordinary prevalence of mercury in common usage during the span of his lifetime. If you read this book, you may come to believe, as I do, that Lewis Carroll's Mad Hatter was based on a man he knew intimately well, *himself*, and that not only did he suffer from mercury poisoning, but it was very likely the cause of many of his early disabilities— his deafness and the stammer which afflicted so many of his siblings—as well as the cause of the ailments that afflicted the author in his later years, his problems with his gait, his introversion, and increasing emotional problems, his insomnia, migraines, epileptiform fits and his eventual untimely death. It may seem fantastic that such a claim could be made regarding the life of a man so closely studied as Lewis Carroll, a life in which every word the man has written or which has been written about him has been pored over, again and again. But that very closeness of study is what has caused so many to overlook what seems a natural vein of investigation into the life of the creator of the Mad Hatter.

We are borne—like a leaf which has fallen from a tree into a river—into a world already in progress. We are the leaf, but our lives are also defined by the world we pass through. In my act of pulling back to examine the life of Lewis Carroll, to see the time in which he lived, I have chosen the artifice of beginning with the year in which Carroll's father was born. Charles Dodgson the senior was born in the first year of the new century, in the year 1800, in Hamilton, Lanarkshire, in the lowlands of Scotland. In the year 1800, King George III, the beloved King of the British Empire, was enjoying a long and welcome period of sanity in between his bouts of madness, Napoleon had crossed the Alps and invaded Italy, Thomas Jefferson had just been elected as the 3rd President of the United States, and George Washington was fresh in his grave, having died in December of the previous year, taken suddenly by cynanche trachealis, or "acute laryngitis."

Washington's nephew had seen him only a few days before his death, and thought that he looked well. "It was a bright frosty morning," Washington's nephew wrote later, "he had taken his usual ride, and the clear healthy flush of his cheek, and his sprightly manner, brought the remark from both of us that we had never seen the General look so well." On Friday, December the 13th, Washington went to bed with a "trifling" cold and a sore throat. The next morning he was quite unwell. His attendant, Tobias Lear, related that he found Washington "breathing with difficulty, and hardly able to utter a word." A hot mixture of molasses, vinegar and butter had been prepared to soothe Washington's throat, but "he could not swallow a drop; whenever he attempted it he was distressed, convulsed, and almost suffocated." Word was sent for a doctor, first for Dr. Craik, and then, to make sure someone came as soon as possible, Dr. Brown, who had been recommended by Craik in case of his absence.

Craik and Washington had served long years together in battle, Washington in various levels of command, and Craik as an army surgeon. They had become friends and their friendship had survived their more comfortable years as well. Just that past year, Washington had appointed Craik as the Surgeon General of the United States. Craik soon arrived to attend to his dear old friend. He bled Washington, and gave him "two moderate doses" of the mercurial compound calomel, and a suppository "which operated on the lower intestines", and sent for his colleague Dr. Dick. When Dick and Brown arrived, they consulted with Dr. Craik. Washington's attendant Tobias Lear reported that the physicians left the room as a group and that Dr. Craik returned and administered calomel. Dr. Craik's report, co-authored with Elisha Dick, differed somewhat. He reported that "one of" the consulting physicians gave Washington "ten grains of calomel." The bleeding and the calomel had "no effect" and Washington died a hard death before the day was through.[1]

Questions raised 60 years later as to whether Washington's physicians had brought about his death by the injudicious

---

[1] Life of George Washington, Weld Horatio Hastings (1811-1888) 1845, Philadelphia, Lindsay and Blakiston, pp190-197; Lear's account was set down on the day following Washington's death; Fac similes of Letters from his excellency George Washington, President of the United States of America, to Sir John Sinclair, Bart., M.P. 1844, Washington, Published by Franklin Knight, Appendix 1, An Official and Particular Account of the Illness and Death of the Illustrious Washington, as published by the physicians who attended him. Pp. 69-71. United States. Congress., . (18341856). *The Debates and proceedings in the Congress of the United States.* Washington: Gales and Seaton. History of Congress, 1799-1801, The Death of General Washington, Dec 15, 1799 statement by Tobias Lear and official Statement of James Craik and Elisha Dick. The Debates and Proceedings in the Congress of the United States, Sixth Congress Dec 1799 to Mar 1801, 1851, Washington, Printed and published by Gales and Seaton. P 206

administration of excessive amounts of calomel, were "answered" by the comment that the physicians' actions had been consistent with the standard practice of the time. Investigating physicians acknowledged an "unwillingness not to think well of Dr. Craik, who was the personal friend of Washington through his life." He had done as well as any of his critics would have done, they judged, as the use of mercurials in inflammatory disease was "very common" in the United States in 1799.

> In 1799 the use of mercurials in inflammatory disease was very rare, I believe, in Great Britain, though it was very common in this country. At the present day [1860] the reverse is true. At least in New England the practice is now relied on much less than in old England. Fashions change, it must be acknowledged, in medicine as in other things.[2]

In 1800, the year in which Charles Dodgson the senior was born, the use of mercury as an internal remedy in England *was on the rise*. For almost 100 years physicians in *New* England had been using mercury in fevers of every description. American physicians were, in fact, so sold on the efficacy of mercury, that they often administered it to their patients without their knowledge, in order to safeguard their popularity, as the people had strong prejudices against mercury.[3] And with good reason, as some forms of it, especially the bichloride of mercury, known as

---

[2] Jackson, J. (1861). *Another letter to a young physician: to which are appended some other medical papers.* Boston: Ticknor and Fields. Pp 176-177

[3] *"The fullest confidence was reposed in a moderate course of mercury in pleurisies and peripneumonies, esteeming it as the most efficacious attenuant and expectorant which the material medica afforded. But the strongest prejudices against the use of mercury subsisted among all classes of people, and physicians were obliged to observe the utmost caution in its administration, as their popularity depended upon concealment."* American Medical Biography: or Memoirs of Eminent Physicians who have flourished in America. James Thatcher, M.D., Boston, Richardson & Lord and Cottons & Barnard, 1828, p 28

mercuric chloride or corrosive sublimate, were highly poisonous. It had been discovered, however, that combining mercuric chloride (a chemical compound formed of mercury and chlorine) with liquid mercury would produce a more mild compound known as calomel (or mercurous chloride). In England doctors were just beginning to rely on the use of calomel in preference to bleeding. The older doctors who had spent years bleeding weren't sure this was a good thing, but with every year that passed more and more of them fell in line, especially in the treatment of children, the *majority* of whom had routinely died after a course of aggressive bleeding. "These circumstances," English physicians held, "rendered it fair to make a trial of the practice of giving calomel." By the year 1800, many practitioners had altogether abandoned bleeding in childhood diseases, and relied entirely on calomel, given in large and repeated doses.

The English physicians had been encouraged to let go of old methods by the astonishing success of Dr. Edward Jenner's new method of inoculation against small pox, an ancient and deadly disease with high mortality rates which often left those who survived disfigured by scarring for life. Jenner had diligently investigated and proven something which had already been understood by local dairy farmers for many years, that those who were exposed to the bovine cow pox virus attained full to partial immunity from the deadly human small pox virus.

In 1798 Jenner had published his findings, Informing the world that his experiments had proven that cowpox—an eruption that appeared frequently on the udders of cows—appeared to lend protection against small pox to those who handled the udders and teats. Inoculation, the act of introducing the cow pox virus in order to create immunity against small pox virus, was a simple matter of exposing a cut or scratch on the arm to matter taken from a cow pox cyst. For the next 8 to 10 years, clergymen, midwives, parents, and other community care takers stepped forward to assist with widespread efforts to inoculate the populace, with great success.[4]

Some people reacted very negatively to the idea of introducing an animal disease into the human body, however, and many of those proceeded with a different form of inoculation, that of matter taken from the small pox cyst of a person who had experienced a *mild* form of the disease. Because this was potentially a very dangerous thing to do, much attention was given to those factors which seemed to lead to the desired outcome—a mild, survivable and non-disfiguring case of the disease. One observable factor in favor of a mild case of the disease was the state of the constitution of the person receiving the infection.[5] Another was mercury. Just as the dairy farmers had claimed that those exposed to cow pox did not come down with small pox, the Germans claimed that small pox never visited areas where mercury was mined, leading many, and especially the Germans, to believe that "calomel was effective in preventing infection, or at least in causing it to be mild and safe."[6] As soon as smallpox appeared in the neighborhood, it was common practice for those who were not yet infected to begin preparing the body to handle the infection by taking calomel "as the physician might judge proper, every night and morning."[7]

---

[4] The Home Book of Health and Medicine: A Popular Treatise on the means of avoiding and curing diseases, by a physician of Philadelphia, Philadelphia, Key & Biddle, 1834, p412

[5] Ibid, p 409

[6] The adoption of Inoculation for Smallpox in England and France, Genevieve Miller, Philadelphia, University of Philadelphia Press, 1957 pp 41-42, Citing Fuller, Exanthematologia; or an attempt to give a rational account of eruptive fevers, especially of the Measle and Small-pox, &c., Thomas Fuller, M.D. London, 1730, pp 188, 194

[7] A Practical Essay on the Small-Pox, William Hillary, M.D., London, 1740 Pp 58-59

This was called an "alterative," a medicine intended to "gradually" and "imperceptibly" improve the constitution of the body, and the medicine most frequently used for that purpose was mercury.   Doctors routinely administered a preparatory course of mercury for some period of time before small pox inoculations as well, and "the preparatory treatment lasted commonly a month."[8] Later physicians began to believe that if the use of mercury could mitigate the severity of small pox, a full course would absolutely prevent the disease.[9]

> ...most of those practitioners, who for upwards of half a century have had extensive experience in the Small Pox, have employed calomel; some believing it to be the preferable purge; others conceiving it to be beneficial on other grounds.   But their agreeing almost universally to prescribe it, affords a presumption, that calomel, by some action, mitigates the variolous fever."[10]

In 1805, the Scottish physician Andrew Duncan published *The Edinburgh New Dispensatory* which brought together in one volume the combined pharmaceuticals of the 1791 *London Pharmacopoeia*, the 1794 *Dublin Pharmacopoeia*, and the 1803 *New Edition of the Edinburgh Pharmacopoeia*.   Duncan's compilation included, not only the information contained in the previous pharmacopoeias, but also an expanded and updated section on mercury, or quicksilver (routinely referred to by the latin variation of Hydrargyrum in Dublin, and Hydrarygyrus in London and Edinburgh.) The newly expanded section began with a history and general overview which read as follows:

---

[8] The History of the Small Pox, by James Moore, London, Longman, Hurst, Rees, Orme and Brown, 1815 p 264-265
[9] Ibid, pp 273-274
[10] Ibid p 293, emphasis added.

There are considerable mines of mercury in Hungary and in Spain; and what is employed in England is principally imported from the former country. Mercury taken into the stomach in its metallic state has no action on the body, except what arises from its weight or bulk. It is not poisonous as was vulgarly supposed, but perfectly inert. But in its various states of combination, it produces certain sensible effects. It quickens the circulation, and increases all the secretions and excretions. According to circumstances, the habit of the body of the patient, the temperature in which he is kept, the nature of the preparation, and the quantity in which it is exhibited, its effects are indeed various; it sometimes increases one secretion more particularly, sometimes another, but its most characteristic effect is the increased flow of saliva, which it generally excites if given in sufficient quantity.[11]

The many and varied preparations of mercury—purified, ground into a fine powder and mixed with oily or sweet substances or carbonate of lime, oxidized by nitrous acid and combined with muriatic acid, acetous acid, or sulphur by sublimation (conversion from a gas to a solid or vice versa) or by precipitation (the mixture of fine particles into a liquid solution)— were listed as "exhibited" for the following medical uses, [definitions of obscure medical terms have been provided in brackets[12]]; as a stimulant; as an antispasmodic, as an errhine [a drug to stimulate nasal discharge], as a sialogogue [a drug to stimulate salivation], as a cathartic [a drug to cause emptying of the bowels], as a diuretic [a drug causing increased urine output], as a sudorific [a drug to stimulate sweating], as an emmenagogue [a drug used to bring on menstruation], as an astringent [a

---

[11] The Edinburgh New Dispensatory, by Andrew Duncan, M.D., First Worcester Edition, Worcester, Isaiah Thomas, 1805, pp 233-234

[12] The definition of terms not appearing in current medical dictionaries. Such as errhine, emmenagogue, and ague, have been taken from Medical Lexicon, A Dictionary of Medical Science, by Robley Dunglison, M.D., Philadelphia, Blanchard and Lea, 1856.

substance that draws tissues, such as pores, together], and as an anthelmintic [a drug that destroys or expels intestinal parasitic worms].

Mercury was used "frequently", but not always; in febrile diseases [fevers]; in obstinate agues [an intermittent fever, believed to be malarial], in inflammatory diseases; in indolent and chronic inflammations, especially of the glandular viscera, as the liver, spleen, &c., in exanthematous diseases [a skin rash as the result of infectious disease, such as measles or scarlet fever]; variola [small pox], in profluvia; in dysentery [an intestinal affliction marked by severe diarrhea], in spasmodic diseases; tetanus [a bacterial disease causing severe neck and jaw spasm], trismus [jaw spasm characteristic of early stage of tetanus], hydrophobia [rabies], &c., in cachectic diseases [diseases causing weakness, loss of appetite, weight loss and muscle wasting]; anasarca [edema, fluid build up], ascites [fluid build up in the abdomen], hydrothorax [build up of fluid in the chest cavity], hydrocephalus [build up of fluid around the brain], &c., in impetigines [contagious skin infection caused by staphylococcal or streptococcal bacteria], in scrofula[tuberculosis of lymph glands], syphilis, lepra, icterus [jaundice], &c., and in local diseases such as caligo corneae [an affliction of the membrane of the eye], amaurosis [impairment of vision with no obvious cause], and gonorrhea.

In other words, mercury might be used in almost any illness. But, as was always the case with mercury in the 1800's, there was no critic who did not admit some advantage to the use of mercury, and no advocate who did not allow for its dangers. Duncan's New Dispensatory included warnings that mercury could cause violent purging of the bowels, "even of blood", an effect to be remedied by "intermitting" the use of the medicine. In the case of severe inflammation of the mouth with excessive salivation "the mercury must be discontinued *for a time.*" Also to be watched for, a potentially fatal sensitization to mercury termed "erethismus" characterized by extreme weakness, a sense of anxiety, depression, trembling, a fast weak pulse, and a sense of coldness. In this state, a sudden physical exertion could prove fatal, requiring that the use of mercury be discontinued, whatever the stage or violence of the disease for which it had been employed.[13]

In 1811, James Wilson, an assistant apothecary of Guy's Hospital in London put together a second edition of his *Manual of Chirurgical [Surgical] Pharmacy*, including a section on mercury taken nearly word for word from *Duncan's Dispensatory*, referring to it "as appearing to us more practical than any other we have seen."[14] What Wilson added gives up a picture in time of mercury's rise in medicine when he states that of the many and various forms of mercury, the submuriate of mercury, or calomel, "is more extensively, and perhaps more usefully, employed by the surgeon than that of any other article in the Materia Medica...whether administered as a purgative, or given as an alterative..."[15] The first printing of the *Manual of Chirurgical [Surgical] Pharmacy* sold out, and second and third editions were printed, including Amercian editions. Mercury was officially sanctioned, the go-to drug.

Dr. Hamilton, the English physician most responsible for the adoption of American style mercurial therapies by the English, recommended that children with croup be given calomel every hour until their breathing eased, after which dosing should

---

[13] Ibid, p 236.

[14] Pharmacopoeia Chirurgica: Or, A Manual of Chirurgical Pharmacy, comprising all the valuable formulae of the New London Pharmacopoeia, and of the several pharmacopoeias appertaining to this branch of science, J. Wilson, London, E. Cox, 1811, p 115.

[15] P 121.

continue, but at gradually longer intervals, "allowing at first two, then three, and finally four or five hours to intervene between each dose according to the state of the symptoms." One to two grains per dose for a child under the age of 1 year, two to three grains for a child over the age of 1 but under the age of 2, three to four grains per dose for a child over the age of 2 but under the age of 4, and five to six grains per dose for a child over the age of 4 but under the age of 6, or, in other words, more calomel for the average child with croup than had been given to General Washington.

Dyspepsia, the Rise of a Bilious Sickness

Sovereign cure of visceral ill,
Pride of Pharmacy, Blue Pill!

-Sir Robert Dallas

Those children who survived their early childhood diseases—including the then 10 year old Charles Dodgson the senior—would have been fascinated by the story of *The Incredible Fasting Woman of Tutbury*, a woman who claimed that she had taken no food or liquid by mouth for more than two years. The woman, Ann Moore, had become quite famous, attracting visitors from all over the United Kingdom. The story she told was that after attending a sick man, she had completely lost her appetite for food. "What little food she did take, she swallowed with difficulty, and suffered, for the space of one or two hours afterwards, the most agonizing pain in the region of the stomach. The severity of the pain sometimes threw her into convulsions." For a great while she ate only bread washed down with water or tea without milk or sugar, and of that, no more than a small loaf every two weeks. She kept on that way for two years, her limbs emaciated, her abdomen sunken up into her ribs, and subject to insomnia and constant pain of the face and right side of her body. After two years in this state, she often suffered reactive convulsions brought on "from so slight an excitement as surprize."

When the Reverend Legh Richmond, Rector of Turvey in Bedford, dropped by in the year 1810 to observe her state, Ann Moore told him that she could not swallow without the danger of suffocation, and that she felt neither appetite nor thirst. Somewhere along the line she began to claim that she was not eating or drinking *anything, not at any time*. We cannot know her motives, but it appears likely that Ann Moore, an obviously ill and impoverished single mother raising two children, began to appreciate the possibility that she might be able to exploit her situation for financial gain.

Reverend Richmond set up a "Watch" to observe Ann Moore and to verify the truthfulness of her story. As far as the members of the Watch could see, Ann Moore took no food or liquid for a period of *three weeks*. Reverend Richmond's unfortunately credulous speculation that the woman might be absorbing nutrients from the surrounding atmosphere brought *The Incredible Fasting Woman of Tutbury* national fame.[16] "Multitudes of visitors from all parts of the kingdom" swarmed Tutbury to see her for themselves. Two years later, when the Rev. Richmond returned with his colleagues, the Rev. Shiply, Vicar of Ashbourne, and a Mr. Collin from London, Richmond found a much more self-important woman, an effect "which was ascribed to the effects of so extensive and singular a kind of popularity as she had obtained amongst her numerous visitors from all parts of the kingdom."

A committee of *19* men was then formed to watch Ann Moore for a period of *four* weeks, an extension of time which caused her initially to refuse the Watch. Eventually, she grudgingly agreed, stating, "I never should have refused your proposal, if I had not thought it proceeded from those who wish me ill, and whom nothing ever would persuade of my integrity. But you are welcome to watch me for four weeks, and when you have done that, for six months longer, if you are willing." She was, however,

---

[16] The Edinburgh Medical and Surgical Journal, Volume Fifth, Edinburgh, George Ramsey & Company, 1809, XI. Some Account of the Fasting Woman at Titbury [sic], who has at present lived above two years without food, by Benjamin Granger, pp 319-321

soon found to be faking when the watch discovered she was sucking water out of the damp rags used to soothe a fever which had overtaken her. Later it was admitted that in the usual course of her life, Ann Moore's children had often left out a pot of tea with milk and sugar and bread, hoping to tempt their mother to eat and drink *something*, and she clearly had, at least often enough to keep her alive. Ann Moore was a "fake." Nevertheless, her case brought to light other incidences of men and women with tremendous aversion to food, often reported as coming on after some form of fever, injury or illness—insomniacs whose bellies cleaved up to their own backbones—living, breathing skeletons who could not be forced to eat.[17]

These people were said to be suffering from dyspepsia, or bilious fever, an extreme form of nervous indigestion believed to be caused by the failure, or inability, of the liver to secrete sufficient bile to aid in the process of digestion. As such, dyspeptics were commonly placed on a course of mercury to compel the liver to act. Dyspepsia was seen as a spectrum disorder, ranging from the relatively innocuous discomfort of overindulgence to a serious disorder which could torment a person to the point of anorexia, and which could end with agonizing neuralgia, apoplexy and death.

Dyspepsia began with difficulty sleeping, a sense of weakness, nervous irritability and mental despondency. In its early stages, the condition itself could lead to harmful excesses, as the dyspeptic "finds food often supplies the want of sleep," and finds alcohol or opiates help to calm his uneasiness. He has nightmares. His stomach begins to turn on him, he has heartburn, and pain in the stomach and abdomen. Constipation becomes

---

[17] A statement of facts, relative to the supposed abstinence of Ann Moore, Rev Legh Richmond, A.M., J. Croft, London, 1813

chronic, and, as the dyspeptic begins to believe certain types of food are the cause of his distress, his diet narrows. It is not difficult for the dyspeptic to cut back, as his appetite becomes sickly and unpredictable. He loses weight. At length his nerves are affected, and "the troubles and perplexities of life begin to be felt more acutely—little things disturb his tranquility", depression sets in, headaches become migraines. If the condition continues to progress, the dyspeptic develops numbness, tremor and spasm of his muscles, trigeminal neuralgia, high blood pressure and possible death by apoplexy—a hemorrhage in the brain.

Dyspepsia was *the* chronic health issue of the 1800s, and as such, the condition led to a surge of health and regimen books advising small amounts of plain food, fresh air, exercise and sleep, a training regimen for health, including moderation in study and purgative medicines, of which hardly anything could be said to be superior to two grains of calomel compounded with colocynth, made into a pill and taken at bed-time, to be repeated 2 or 3 times as needed to speedily clear the stomach and bowels "thus getting rid of any accumulations that may be oppressing those important organs" and thereby interfering with proper digestion.[18] In time, the calomel would be replaced by a mass produced small dose mercury pill, followed by a saline draught to make sure the medicine moved quickly through the body.

The use of mercury as an after dinner medication to keep indigestion at bay became so commonplace that it probably accounts for the majority of mercury used in the 1800s. Sadly, mercury prescribed in mild cases of dyspepsia with the aim of preventing the progression to a more serious disorder most likely brought about the very problems it was meant to prevent, as

---

[18] Sure methods of improving health, and prolonging life, or, a treatise on the art of living long and comfortably, by regulating the diet and regimen, by Thomas John Graham, London: Simpkin and Marshall, 1827, 2nd ed.

violent pain in the stomach, nerve disorders and anorexia are all known effects of mercury poisoning. But if the mercury prescribed to counteract dyspepsia increased its symptoms in a vicious self-perpetuating cycle, what was the initiating cause that drove sufferers to seek medical care in the first place? The likely culprit was arsenic and mercury used in animal husbandry. In the early 1800s, arsenic dips and baths were routinely given to farm animals each autumn in an effort to control pests. Arsenic clears from the body fairly quickly, but it often happened that the animals which had sickened and died from over aggressive treatment were butchered and sent to market.[19] Eventually concerns over arsenic in meat would prompt a switch to mercurial treatments, not so quickly deadly, but still capable of causing great harm through food chain contamination.

Consider the following fictionalized memoir relating the experience of dyspepsia. Reading the passage, you can see that the author believed, as did so many people of the time, that dyspepsia was due to over-indulgence, but, seen from an outside perspective, it is clear that something was *wrong* with the meat:

Things are different now. We have suppers that are solid substantial matters. Quarters of mutton, cut into wedges, and rounds of beef carved into respectable steaks, fly before us. Our suppers, in fact, are things which are felt at the moment, and for some time afterwards. You go to bed stupid, sleep with the nightmare, and get up with a headache. You try to read the paper, and you go over a very interesting leader, and a speech

---

[19] Clater, F. (1814). *Every man his own cattle doctor.* London: E. and H. Hodson. P 340; Tessier, A. Henri. (1811). *A complete treatise on merinos and other sheep ..: Recently published at Paris.* New-York: Printed at the Economical School Office [by Joseph Desnoues]. pp 106-107; Katherine Golden Bitting,. (1810). *The Family receipt-book, or, Universal repository of useful knowledge and experience in all the various branches of domestic economy.* London: Oddy and Co., p 94

of your favourite member, without understanding a word of either. Within your brain all is chaos, your thoughts are confused, and there is a revolution in your stomach. You consult your pill-box, and order a neck of mutton. Broth is your only consolation—Calomel and colocynth your best friends. You cannot bear to look a sheep or an ox in the face—even the old cow in the meadow causes painful reminiscences. You walk about that day like a resuscitated corpse—your chin unshorn, your face grimy, your hair dusty, your eyes half shut, your tongue white or brown, your hand shaking, and your whole self bedeviled. A day or two brings you round, and at it you go again. This is life in "our town."[20]

The following excerpt of the poem, *Written During a Bilious Sickness* by Jonathon Douglas, contains a first person account of the experience of a "bilious" sickness. The first stanza makes it clear that the author has experienced multiple bouts of bilious sickness, and blames the onset of his episodes on both over-indulgence and too much mental excitement. The remaining stanzas detail the symptoms of bilious sickness; the discomfort caused by eating, headache, pain and nausea, temperature deregulation, increased pulse, giddiness, tremor, limb pain, fatigue, depression and anxiety, hallucination, and eventual extreme weight loss.

Written During a Bilious Sickness[21]

This bilious sickness turns me sallow,
If I a sauce or gravy swallow,
Pie, pudding, or a stew;

---

[20] Our town; or, rough sketches of character, manners, &c. by Peregrine Reedpen, Vol II, London, 1834
[21] Miscellaneous Poems, Jonathon Douglas, Mayport, Printed by Robert Adiar, and sold by Whittaker and Co., London; and Rancks and Co., Manchester, 1836

Or take a glass, get in a passion,
Which is I own too much my fashion,
I soon have cause to rue.

And when the burning fit comes on,
Before the peep of early dawn,
My throbbing temples ache;
In all the regions of the brain,
I feel, in dreams, a real pain,
And with the nausea wake.

An icy coldness chills the feet,
While intermittent cold and heat,
Thrill every nerve and vein;
The feverish pulse beats hard and quick,
The heart grows faint, the stomach sick,
And retchings rive the brain.

A giddy darkness round me swims,
A shivering seizes all the limbs,
An aching every bone;
A drowsiness—but not of sleep,
Steals on me, and the senses steep
In lethargy alone.

Unbidden tears come in my eyes,
And deep involuntary sighs,
Of visionary woes:
While sudden dread, but not of fear,
Comes o'er me when no danger's near;
And starts without a cause.

The spirits then forget to flow,
Strange phantoms pass in mimic show,
And fate seems hovering near;

But there's a hand the wound to cure,
To guard me in the trying hour,
And wipe off every tear.

The Doctor's come—I'm all belief,
But find in physic no relief,
Yet still the dose repeat;
And after all their skill can do,
I feel the throbbing in my brow,
And almost hear it beat.

To hear the cant and see the fuss,
With dubious words to cozen us,
Mysterious looks and nods;
Like oracles, whose words convey
A double meaning—either way,
Can make but little odds.

My body like a shadow grows,
Where wind as through a blanket blows,
Until I'm in a shiver;
And then I heap on warmer clothes,
Wry faces make, and take a dose,
Which salivates the liver.

For I've been dos'd and drugg'd enough,
With powders, antibilious stuff,
Pills, calomel, and slop,
Till thus reduced to what you see,
A living stuff'd anatomy,
A walking druggist shop.

The author of *Written During a Bilious Sickness* specifically mentions that physicians have given him calomel for his biliousness, so it is not too surprising that the symptoms he details are so closely aligned with those of mercury poisoning: headache, gastric pain, cold extremities, fast pulse, tremor, fatigue, depression, nameless anxieties, and extreme weight loss. Mercury poisoning is a well-known cause of personality changes, hypertension, cold, pain and numbness in the extremities and anorexia. What was known at the time, but is little known today, is that those who *recovered* from serious mercury poisoning often found that their appetites not only returned, but often grew strong enough in recovery as to cause the once ill to grow *remarkably fat.*[22]

---

[22] "In all severe cases, the appetite fails, and emaciation proceeds to a very great extent; but it is a remarkable fact, that many patients who have suffered severely from the effects of mercury become afterwards remarkably fat." Coley, J. Milman. (1846). *A practical treatise on the diseases of children.* London: Printed for Longman, Brown, Green, & Longmans, p. 149

Robert Waring Darwin on the Watch

*He was about 6 feet 2 inches in height, with broad shoulders,
and very corpulent, so that he was the largest man whom I ever
saw. When he last weighed himself, he was 24 stone, but
afterwards increased much in weight.*

-Charles Darwin on Dr. R. W. Darwin

One of the men on watch to determine the truthfulness or deceit of the anorexic Ann Moore was the hugely fat high society physician, Robert Waring Darwin. Darwin had set up practice in the pretty little town of Shrewsbury at the tender age of 22 armed only with a small start-up fund and the 2nd volume of his father's *Zoonomia, or the Laws of Organic Life*. His father, Erasmus Darwin, had been a well-known high society physician in the nearby midlands town of Derby who had made a reputation for himself through the use of "an entirely novel course of treatment" considered by many to be "rash, experimental" and "theoretical." Erasmus Darwin was *not* a man to stand back and wait for the consensus of his colleagues, a criticism that might well have enhanced his reputation as the man to call when desperate measures were required. He had a face which bore the ravages of a severe case of small pox, as did so many others of his generation, and he was prepared to do everything possible to fight that disease. He was an early and enthusiastic proponent of inoculation against small pox, and a strong believer in a full course of mercurial treatments, using mercury to "prepare" the body for inoculation, as a treatment during the course of the disease to render it more mild, and as an external treatment to render the pustules less likely to scar. This could be accomplished by spreading the inside of a thin leather mask with a mercurial ointment and leaving it in place for three or four days.[23]

Erasmus Darwin turned the full attention of his medical theory to the two great sorrows of his life, the long term ill health of his wife, and the intractable stammering of his oldest son, Charles. Erasmus' wife had been ill from the beginning of their marriage until her death 13 years later. As his biographer said, "The potent skill, and assiduous cares of him, before who disease daily vanished from the frame of others, could not expel it radically from that of her he loved. It was however kept at bay thirteen years."[24] The means used are not mentioned, but we cannot ignore that in *Zoonomia* Erasmus Darwin repeatedly recommended mercurial cures, both as an alterative, to improve the constitution, and as a specific, to address existing illnesses. Knowing that Mrs. Darwin was likely kept on a strong mercurial course for the duration of her illness renders the following letter written before her death especially poignant,

Do not weep for my impending fate. In the short term of my life, a great deal of happiness has been comprised. The maladies of my frame were peculiar; the pains in my head and stomach, which no medicine could eradicate, were spasmodic and violent; and required stronger measures to render them supportable while they lasted, than my constitution could sustain without injury. The periods of exemption from those pains were frequently of several days duration, and in my intermissions, I felt no indication of malady. Pain taught me the value of ease, and I enjoyed it with a glow of spirit, seldom, perhaps, felt by the habitually healthy.[25]

---

[23] Chase, A. W. 1817-1885. (1888). *Dr. Chase's recipes: or, Information for everybody: an invaluable collection of about eight hundred practical recipe*, Ann Arbor, Mich.: R. A. Beal., p 363.

[24] Seward A, (1804) Memoirs of the Life of Dr. Darwin, London, J. Johnson, p12

[25] Ibid, p 13.

That Erasmus Darwin may, by his own actions, have been responsible for the death of his beloved wife is incredibly tragic. But consider this—Erasmus' wife bore 5 children during the course of her long term illness, and they would, each of them, have been exposed to the mercury taken prior to, and possibly during, her pregnancies. As difficult as it is for us to believe, women of the time *did* take mercurial medication while they were pregnant,[26] and when a woman is exposed to mercury during pregnancy, the baby she carries is exposed to an even *greater* degree, as the body uses the fetus in an attempt to expel the toxin from the mother's system. Not surprisingly, two of Erasmus' children died in infancy. The oldest boy, Charles (the brother of Robert Waring Darwin, and therefore the uncle of the famous naturalist Charles Darwin), had "contracted" his father's propensity to stammer. Although we now know that mercury exposure can cause neuropathological changes in the brain that can cause impairment—stammering, hesitation or thickening—of speech, this was not widely known at the time.

For quite some time stammering had been blamed on various defects in the physical conformity of the mouth, such as the size of the tongue and the frenum (the little band of tissue connecting the tongue to the floor of the mouth), as well as poorly arranged teeth, or inflexible lips, and surgeons had set out on a series of horrifying experiments cutting wedges from the root of the tongue, and removing the tonsils or uvula, and so forth, but the failure of these efforts forced the consideration of other causes. One French physician, M. Voison, a stammerer himself, came to the conclusion that "stammering depends on a disorder of the cerebral functions... an imperfect reaction of the brain on the

---

[26] The Transsylvania Journal of Medicine and the Associate Sciences, Edited by Lunsford P. Yandell, M.D., Vol VI, Lexington, Kentucky, 1833, Cooke on Cholera, p355

organs of speech." Physical conformation could not explain some of the stranger aspects of stammering, such as "why stammerers, in general, sing without effort, and harangue with fluency..."[27] Or why, for that matter, Erasmus Darwin could speak more clearly when drunk... for Erasmus had a terrible problem with stammering himself.

Popular opinion as to the cause of this disorder in the brain was somewhat evenly divided between heredity and the sort of "sensitive" and "imaginative" temperament which could be derailed by an idea, one in whom stammering could begin by hearing or imitating a stammer, a stammer caught, like a virus, and made permanent "by some strange inner reaction on his nerves of volition."[28] Erasmus Darwin was such a strong believer in imitative stammering that he sent his son away to live in France in an attempt to cure his stammer. Erasmus believed that "in the pronunciation of a foreign language, hesitation would be less likely to recur, than in speaking those words and sentences, in which [Charles] had been accustomed to hesitate." Charles was sent away at age 12 under direction that he not be allowed to converse in English at all. After 2 years in France, away from the stammering (and mercurial) influences of his father, Charles came back cured of the worst of his stammering, although "his utterance was, from that time, somewhat thick and hurried."[29]

---

[27] The Medical Intelligencer: or Monthly Compendium of Medical, Chirurgical, and Scientific Knowledge, Vol III for 1822, London, Burgess and Hill, review of On the nature and causes of Stammering, by Felix Voisin, pp 89-91

[28] Fraser's Magazine for Town and Country, Vol LX, July, 1859, The Irrationale of Speech, by a Minute Philosopher, p 5, "A Minute Philosopher" is identified as the phrenonym of the Revered Charles Kingsley in the papers Hints to Stammerers, and The Irrationale of Speech, subscribed C.K. and printed in Fraser's Magazine, July, 1859, Handbook for Fictitious Names, by Olphar Hamst, London, John Russell Smith, 1868

[29] Seward A, (1804) Memoirs of the Life of Dr. Darwin, London, J Johnson, p 62-3

It was at this time that Erasmus Darwin began working on his *Zoonomia,* the first volume of which expounded on Erasmus Darwin's theory of the heritability of characteristics acquired during a creature's lifespan, the driving force of which was an irritation brought about by *imitation* and *imagination*. He wrote in illustration that "examples of these irritative imitations are daily observable in common life; thus one yawning person shall set a whole company yawning; and some have acquired winking of the eyes or impediments of speech by imitating their companions without being conscious of it."[30] Erasmus Darwin's theories would later be dismissed as "erroneous" by his grandson, Charles Darwin, the great naturalist and father of the theory of evolution as we now know it, but they are helpful in understanding the blurry line that existed at the time between heritability and imitation in the field of stammering research. At the time, Erasmus Darwin's theories were considered to be "ingenious, beyond all precedent."[31]

The second volume of *Zoonomia* summarized the "gathered wisdom" of Darwin's 23 years of medical practice, and it was this volume which Erasmus' son Robert referred to in his own practice of medicine. *Zoonomia* recommended calomel for worms, obstructed bowel, failure of the natural motion of the intestinal canal, as an alterative, for small pox, for diseases of sensation and volition, for anorexia with epileptic fits, for convulsions, for nervous rheumatism in the legs, for paralysis of the liver, and for madness.[32] "Calomel," Erasmus Darwin had written in *Zoonomia*, "given in the dose from ten or twenty grains, so as to induce purging without the assistance of other drugs, appears to me to particularly increase the secretion of bile and to evacuate it." He

---

[30] Zoonomia, Vol 1 pp. 204-205. Check vol date and page no placement.
[31] Seward A, (1804) Memoirs of the Life of Dr. Darwin, London, J Johnson, p 85-6
[32] Zoonomia, Vol II, Pp 38, 53, 181-183, 235, 247, 270, 272

believed that an inert state of bile due to failure of the liver to properly act was the cause of many ailments. It was a modern spin on ancient Aristotlean teachings, and a belief which would soon become commonplace throughout all of England.

"Those instructions which, through the channel of its' pages, flow to the world, enabled Dr. Robert Darwin of Shrewsbury to attain instance eminence as a physician in that county, at his first outsetting, and in the bloom of scarcely ripened youth; to continue a course of practice, which has been the blessing of Shropshire; it's sphere expanding with his growing fame." For if Erasmus Darwin's son Charles had "contracted" his propensity to stammer, his son Robert had "contracted" his voracious appetite and enormous size. Robert Waring Darwin practiced in Shrewsbury for 50 years, and in that time, he became so enormously fat that he completely filled his carriage, and had to send a servant on ahead to test the soundness of floors.[33]

---

[33] Meteyard, E. (1871) A group of Englishmen, London, Longmans, Green, and Co., p 263

John Keats and Calomel Curry

Can death be sleep, when life is but a dream?

-John Keats

In 1815, when Charles Dodgson the senior was 15 years old, Robert Darwin's son Charles was only 6. This Charles would become the great naturalist Charles Darwin, and he would also endure the stammering which plagued his uncle and grandfather. In that same year, a twenty year old John Keats—destined to become one of the most well-known of the English Romantic poets—entered medical school at Guy's hospital in London. While there he would have sat for the lectures of "Calomel Curry", a professor at Guy's who had earned his nickname by his passionate enthusiasm for the use of mercury in the restoration of liver function. Curry believed that liver function was of such elemental importance in cases of ill health, that it "saves both physician and patient time to begin straight away with restoration of hepatic function." Yes, he admitted, when mercury was used, "the appetite diminishes, and a degree of languor and weakness is felt over every inch of the body," but as long the patient would take care *not to get cold* during the period in which he was suffering the ill effects of the mercurial treatment, he would soon find his appetite and strength improved to a level *even better* than that which he had experienced before he had taken ill. It was said that "With Curry there was only one organ discussed—the liver; and only one medicine to be prescribed—calomel." It was also said that "Curry sprinkled calomel on the meat of the sandwiches which he ate for luncheon, for he always believed he was laboring under a disease of the liver."[34] Curry had been meaning, for years, to write a proper treatise on liver function and its role in disease, but ill health had prevented him from completing his task.[35] For Calomel Curry was nearly constantly ill.

Keats was also often ill. His mother had died of pulmonary consumption when he was only 14 years old, a tragedy which might have led to his interest in medicine, but in the end, his heart wasn't completely in it, and he would give up medicine to devote himself to his true passion, which was writing. He moved in with his brother George to both start his new life, and to help care for their brother Tom, who had contracted the same form of consumption which had killed their mother.

There was a belief, in that time in the world, that there was some kind of mysterious affinity between pulmonary consumption and the poetic mind. It seemed to them as if poets and literary men were affected by the disease more often than other men. Trying to puzzle this out, doctors of the age came to believe that pulmonary consumption increased mental activity, either because of "the stimulating effect upon the faculties of the toxin generated by the disease process" or because the victims were liable to work with feverish haste to accomplish something worthwhile before they died.[36]

And this certainly happened with Keats as well. He grew ill himself fairly quickly after beginning the care of his brother (who wouldn't live much more than a year longer), and treated himself with mercury, writing, "The little mercury I have taken has corrected the poison and improved my health, though I feel, from

---

[34] A Biographical History of Guy's Hospital, Samuel Wilks, M.D. and G.T. Bettany, London, New York, Melbourne and Sydney, Ward, Lock, Bowden & Co., 1892, Dr. Curry, pp 2040-207

[35] Examination of the Prejudices Commonly Entertained Against Mercury, James Curry, M.D.F.A.S., London, J. M'Creery, 1809

[36] Wells, W. Augustine. (1959). *A doctor's life of John Keats.* [1st ed.] New York: Vantage Press.

my employment, that I shall never again be secure in robustness."
Past biographers, unfamiliar with the use of mercurial medication
in any except for syphilitic infections have assumed that "the
poison" referred to the unfortunate result of an unknown sexual
encounter, when it was almost certainly what Keats must have
feared might be consumption. There was a "general and strong
commendation" of the use of calomel in pulmonary consumption
at that time.[37] Keats' use of the word "employment" refers to his
"employment" of mercury in the treatment of his illness. In that
case, the meaning of his statement becomes quite clear, that
while he has used mercury as a curative agent, he is questioning
whether it might have done him more harm than good—he fears
that he might have done permanent damage to his health. The
phrase "employment of mercury" was used repeatedly in medical
texts of the time period, as evidenced by the following excerpt:

It is remarkable that, notwithstanding the general and long-
continued employment of mercury, it should not have been
known that all its constitutional effects, not excepting complete
salivation, may generally be obtained by such doses as half or
even the third part of a grain of blue-pill taken three times a
day: that is a dose only equal to the twentieth or thirtieth part of
a grain of calomel; for a grain of calomel is equal, whether we
regard its purgative, or, when divided into minute parts, its
alterative, effects, to ten grains of blue-pill. If such be the case,
what should induce us to employ larger quantities, except the
disease requires a more rapid effect than can be obtained from
such doses, or, from such peculiarity in it or the habit of the
patient, the sensibility to their effects is impaired? No other
person, as far as I know, has been led to the use of these doses

[37] Armstrong, J. (1823). *Facts, observations, and practical illustrations, relative
to puerperal fever, scarlet fever, pulmonary consumption and measles.* 1st
American ed. Hartford: O. D. Cooke & sons., p 131

of mercury, which, I think it will be admitted from the facts I am about to state, constitute, in a great variety of cases, its most beneficial employment.[38]

Keats' old medical school professor, Calomel Curry, used the term "employment of mercury" himself, as in "that family has since lost their child by rejecting the *employment* of mercury."[39] Proof that Keats and his family had an understanding of the workings of mercury similar to that propounded by Curry, can be found in a letter which his brother George wrote to their sister Fanny, as follows,

Before going to bed I thought it prudent to clear my stomach of bile, and took calomel—a cold taken while this is operating on the system frequently proves fatal, it opens the pores of the skin, and allows the inflammation to lay complete hold of one. Not having slept for two nights, I remained dead asleep while water was dripping thro' the ceiling, until it had penetrated thro' all the clothes, the feather bed and the mattrass. The instant I awoke I jumped out of bed, called the servants, and was put into a fresh bed, fully expecting to be laid up, but this morning to my astonishment I find myself well; you see if I can stand water when it nearly floats me in my bed without injury I cannot be born to be drowned.[40]

John Keats *had* contracted his brother Tom's consumption, although he at first denied it, and he spent the next year working in a passionate, feverish daze, remarkably productive and brilliant. In a letter to a friend, he wrote, "I went to the Isle of Wight,

[38] On the Influence of Minute Doses of Mercury, A.P.W. Philip, M.D., London, Henry Renshaw, 1834, p4 emphasis added
[39] Examination of the Prejudices Commonly Entertained Against Mercury, James Curry, M.D.F.A.S., London, J. M'Creery, 1809, emphasis added.
[40] The poetical works and other writings of John Keats, by Harry Buxton Forman, Vol IV, London, Reeves & Turner, 1883, p 392, letter from George Keats to sister Fanny, Jan 30, 1820, emphasis added

thought so much about poetry so long together that I could not get to sleep at night . . . I was too much in solitude, and consequently was obliged to be in continual burning of thought." He *was* treating himself with mercury, and one of the classic symptoms of inorganic mercury poisoning is an insomnia caused by a speeding up of the mental energies.   The salient question, then, the question that has not been asked is, was Keats' brain quickened by the toxins of his disease, or by the toxins of his cure? In 1817, when the 22 year old Keats "was in a state of mental excitement varied with fits of depression" he wrote *Endymion*, a convoluted 4,000 line poem, an allegory of the relationship of man to beauty whose first line is immediately recognizable to nearly all—"A thing of beauty is a joy for ever."[41] The first few lines of Keats' complex Endymion have become a part of our world.

> *A thing of beauty is a joy for ever:*
> *Its loveliness increases; it will never*
> *Pass into nothingness; but still will keep*
> *A bower quiet for us, and a sleep*
> *Full of sweet dreams, and health, and quiet breathing.*

Keats himself was *not* destined for a life full of sweet dreams, or health, or quiet breathing, but dreams within dreams, ill health, and hemorrhage from the lungs. He spent his last years with "his throat chronically sore, his nerves unstrung,"[42] and died in 1821 at the age of 25 from tuberculosis. Keats was preceded in death by James "Calomel" Curry, for whom the following humorous epitaph was crafted,

---

[41] *Poems of John Keats* (1896) edited by G. Thorn Drury, London: Lawrence & Bullen, pp xvi, xxiii

[42] *John Keats, His Life and Poetry, His Friends, Critics and After-Fame*, Sidney Colvin, New York, Charles Scribner's Sons, 1917, pp 358-359

"Siste, Visitor! do not be in a hurry;
Beneath lies interr'd Doctor Calomel Curry;
Whose history proves that "conjectural art"
Oft makes a bad guess of the true peccant part.
Severely afflicted, long time did he shiver,
With symptoms his fancy ascribed to the liver;
Hydrargyrus submur. Was fruitlessly taken,
For Death proved the Doctor his case had mistaken."[43]

---

[43] *The New Monthly Magazine and Universal Register*, 1820 Part I, January to June, London, Henry Colburn and Co., Death Notice for James Curry M.D., senior physician to Guy's hospital and lecturer on the theory and practice of medicine, Feb 1, 1820 P249; Nugae Canorae; or Epitaphian Mementos, in Stonecutter's verse, or the Medici Family of Modern Times, by Unus Quorum, London, Callow and Wilson 1827.

The Madness of Kings and Emperors

April 26ᵗʰ 1821—The Emperor was pretty calm during the night, until about four in the morning, when he said to me with extraordinary emotion: "I have just seen my good Josephine, but she would not embrace me; she disappeared at the moment when I was about to take her in my arms. She was seated there; it seemed to me that I had seen her yesterday evening: she is not changed; still the same—full of devotion to me. She told me that we were about to see each other again, never more to part; she assured me that—did you see her?" I took great care not to say anything which might increase the feverish excitement, too plainly evident to me. I gave him his potion and changed his linen, and he fell asleep; but on awaking, he again spoke to me of the Empress Josephine, and I should only have uselessly irritated him, by telling him that it was only a dream.

-Montholon

By the year 1818, when Charles Dodgson the senior was 18 years old, Napoleon's reign of world domination was over. He had been placed into exile by the English on Saint Helena, a small island under their control in the lonely middle of the South Atlantic Sea. King George III was only peripherally aware of any of it. He had been locked away in a suite of rooms at Windsor Palace for many years, confirmed as mad. He had lost control of his kingdom, and had been placed in the care of Dr. John Willis, the man who, along with his father, had overseen his Majesty's care during his first serious fit of madness. It had, in fact, been John Willis, and not his father, who had been responsible for prescribing an alterative pill containing calomel to the King at that time. [44] Experienced in the care of the insane—who were often known to refuse the medications given to them—Willis directed that an alterative medication be sprinkled over his Majesty's food to keep the royal digestive system running smoothly. This was important, as it was well known that the insane had a high incidence of digestive disorders, a matter which it was critically important to correct, as it was believed to be highly likely that the physical disorder was an initiating cause of the insanity. There *was* an undeniable physical component to the King's illness, and he had, over the last several years, become blind and deaf, and increasingly unable to walk.

Napoleon was beginning to have similar problems. By the year 1818, the 49 year old Napoleon had grown increasingly deaf, and his eyes were easily tired and over sensitive to light. His legs pained him. He had been attended to by an English physician, Dr. Barry Edward O'Meara, but O'Meara was leaving Saint Helena, and Napoleon's illness appeared to be progressing. O'Meara, and many of the physicians who followed, believed that Napoleon's illness was due, in large part, to his defiance of medical advice. On leaving the island, O'Meara wrote the following report on the Emperor's illness:

> *I proposed the use of mercury, but the patient manifested the most lively repugnance; he rejected the use of this medicine under whatever form it might be disguised. . . . At length, on the 11th of June, we managed to overcome his repugnance to mercury, and I obtained his consent to make use of it. He took mercurial pills; he continued this course of medicine until the 15th; I gave him these pills morning and evening, and occasionally administered some purgatives, in order to remove constipation. At the end of six days, I changed the prescription,*

---

[44] Parliament. House of Commons. (1789). Report from the Committee Appointed to Examine the Physicians who have attended His Majesty During His Illness, Touching the present state of His Majesty's Health, ordered to be printed 13th January 1789, pp 54, 58, 62, 68-69, 125-127

and substituted calomel for mercury; but this produced qualms, vomitings, colic, and general uneasiness; and I ceased to employ it. I administered it again on the 19th; it caused the same disorders. I returned to the mercurial preparation, which I administered three times a-day. I interrupted this treatment on the 27th. The apartments are extremely damp: Napoleon had contracted a violent catarrh; he suffered from high fever and great irritation. I again resumed the mercurial course on the 2nd of July, and continued it until the 9th, but it produced no beneficial effect. The salivary glands remained in the same state. The wakefulness and irritation increased; attacks of giddiness became frequent. [45]

After O'Meara's departure, the next physician who examined Napoleon was also convinced that the Emperor should be treated with mercury. Dr. Stokoe wrote:

"I plainly perceived it to be necessary that he should immediately commence a mercurial treatment, and told him, that under this conviction I should propose pills, and would send them to him on my return to the town, with instructions for taking them," but Napoleon refused to take any medicine. [46]

Eventually, as Napoleon seemed adamantly opposed to following the medical advice of the *English* physicians who had attended him, a young *Corsican* physician was contracted to travel to Saint Helena to oversee Napoleon's care. Antommarchi, a 30 year old anatomist, relatively inexperienced in patient care, prepared to take over by consulting with experts in the field. Stokoe followed up on a personal meeting with Antommarchi with a letter reiterating his belief that Napoleon must be convinced to take a course of mercurial medications.

---

[45] Montholon, C. (1847). *History of the captivity of Napoleon at St. Helena, Vol III*. London: H. Colburn, p 33-34

[46] Ibid, p. 72

"I think it sufficient to repeat in general terms what I have already had the pleasure of mentioning to you personally; that is, that all the experiments and observations I have made, or been able to collect, have fully convinced me that mercurial preparations are the only means by which a radical cure can be effected. Mercury is, of all medicines, that which most effectually answers our expectations, provided there be yet no organic injury; and provided it be administered with prudence, and under proper circumstances."

Antommarchi was grateful for their advice. "All," he wrote, "but particularly the venerable James Curry, so celebrated for his labours on hepatitis, answered me with a zeal and kindness that affected me most sensibly. . . . One of the most distinguished pupils of Dr. Curry did not confine himself to recommending to me the use of mercurial preparations; he wished to enable me to judge by my own observation of the efficacy of this specific." This Dr. Curry was, of course, the famed Dr. *Calomel* Curry. Dr. Curry's star pupil took Antommarchi all over London to see the different ways in which mercury could be used in different cases. "I experienced the same kindness and attentions from several other skillful practitioners of London," wrote Antommarchi, "Every one communicated to me the result of his observations, and his own views and ideas on the subject."

Antommarchi arrived on Saint Helena in September of 1819. He examined Napoleon and recommended the use of mercury both *internally* and *externally*, but Napoleon refused it. Antomarrchi continued to propose mercurial preparations, and Napoleon continued to refuse them. Eventually, Antommarchi won a small measure of concession from the once mighty Emperor. While Napoleon continued to refuse to take any pills, he relented regarding the use of *external* medication. "Apply to my exterior all the medicaments you please, I consent to it," Napoleon said. From that time, under the frequent liniments and enemas Antommarchi directed, Napoleon grew far worse, with painful, reddened legs, violent headache, agitation, deep depression and sleeplessness.[47] Eventually, Napoleon could not bear even the lightest solid substance in his stomach, and he began to lose his grip on reality, raving and talking to people who were not there.

Antommarchi began to look for a way to get out of his assignment, which was just as well, as Napoleon had forbidden him to enter his bedroom. Antommarchi and the other physicians gathered in consultation, and agreed that calomel would be the emperor's only hope. Knowing Napoleon would refuse it, they dissolved ten grains of the medicine into a sweetened drink.[48]

May 4th—This morning, the physicians administered a strong dose of calomel: they say that if they had been able to obtain any effect from it sooner, they should have had some hope." – Montholon[49]

---

[47] While the composition of the liniment Antommarchi used is not specified, ointments made with quicksilver and other forms of mercury designed to convey mercury into the body by being rubbed on the skin were common. An ointment composed of equal parts of calomel and cerate was employed in frictions on the abdomen in engorgement of the liver. *London medical and surgical journal, edited by Michael Ryan, M.D..* (1835) London: G. Henderson vol. VII, p 235. More compelling, the 1819 London Medical dictionary recommended mercurial ointments in the case of hepatitis, the diagnosis Antommarchi was working off of Parr, B. (1819). *The London medical dictionary: including, under distinct heads, every branch of medicine ... with whatever relates to medicine in natural philosophy, chemistry, and natural history.* Philadelphia: Mitchell, p 740
[48] Sokoloff, B. (1937). *Napoleon, a doctor's biography.* New York: Prentice-Hall, inc.. pp 208-243, 278
[49] Montholon, C. (1847). *History of the captivity of Napoleon at St. Helena, Vol III.* London: H. Colburn, p 214.

On May 5th, Napoleon died, having amended his will to read that he was murdered by the English. Napoleon was in the habit of giving locks of his hair to friends and family, and his head was shaved upon his death and the hairs distributed. A test of Napoleon's hair conducted in 1961 revealed both arsenic and mercury, leading many to speculate that Napoleon was, in fact, intentionally murdered with arsenic. But that's just how life was in those days—full of arsenic and mercury. And arsenic was on the way out.[50]

---

[50] Sir George Lefevre (1844) An apology for the nerves: or, their influence and importance in health and disease, London, Longman, Brown, Green and Longman, 1844, pp 242-243 "It is positively fatal to a medical man's reputation, to prescribe arsenic to the higher classes—they will not hear of it. There is no means of disguising it. I did succeed, for some time, by writing Solutio Fowleri. . . but it was discovered, and I could not persevere."

The Water Doctors

I had every reason to be grateful for the attention, and to be confident in the skill, of those whose prescriptions had, from time to time, flattered my hopes and enriched the chemist. But the truth must be spoken—far from being better, I was sinking fast.

-Sir Bulwer Lytton

As Charles Dodgson the senior entered Oxford University to study mathematics and the classics, Vincent Priessnitz, the son of a German farmer in the mountains of Austrian Silesia, had decided that the best way to combat his chronic health issues would be to turn away from traditional medicines and to rebuild his constitution by getting closer to nature. Priessnitz, one year older than Dodgson, had a face covered with small pox scars, a feature which, regarded in light of his decision to turn away from traditional medicine, suggests the likelihood that Priessnitz had been treated with mercurial medications (perhaps a factor in his older brother's death of "brain fever" and his father's subsequent blindness). Priessnitz was a brilliant boy, with "unusual abilities, especially an excellent memory, acute perception, and a remarkably vivid and happy power of observation.' He was good at reading and arithmetic, but was always "backwards" at writing, as he found it very difficult to "wield a pen."[51] This lack of fine motor control suggests a neurological degeneration which is typical of mercury exposure.

Talent met inspiration the day Priessnitz, a keen observer of the natural world, saw a young deer—which had been shot—enter a spring and position itself so that its wound was

---

[51] Life of Vincent Priessnitz, Founder of Hyropathy, by Richard Metcalfe, Simpkin, Marshall, Hamilton, Kent & Co., London 1898

submerged in the flowing water. Day to day, he watched the animal repeat this action until it was healed. Experimenting on himself and then on his neighbors, Priessnitz slowly worked out a system of natural healing using water. In the year 1829, Priessnitz began to operate his water cure as a business, and treated 49 patients. As a result, he was charged with treating patients without a license and imprisoned, but seeking appeal, managed to get the verdict suspended and to obtain, in 1831, official permission to conduct a hydropathic establishment.[52] Instead of the use of mercury and other compounds in allopathic medicine as alteratives, antiphlogistics, diuretics, expectorants, and aperients, Priessnitz advised copious water-drinking, hot-air baths, sitz-baths, hot fomentations, douches (standing under a streaming waterfall) and wet sheet packing (a process which, after a time would produce profuse sweating).[53]

Business was good, with patients claiming cure of all manner of miraculous cures, and in the years from Jan 1839 to Dec 1842, Priessnitz treated thousands of patients.[54] Establishments offering similar cures began to open in Germany, France, England and America. Grateful patients claimed miracle cures of chronic conditions, from cures of nervous dyspepsia, to cures of deafness, blindness and paralysis. As one article on the enthusiasm of the water cure patients read, "it appears to verge on the impossible."[55]

There is a well-known quote—attributed to Voltaire—that "the art of medicine consists of amusing the patient while Nature cures the disease." Is it possible that the secret of the water cure was not in the water itself, but in the length of time that the

---

[52] Ibid, p 26
[53] Ibid, pp. 165-167
[54] A Medical Visit to Gräfenberg, by Sir Charles Scudamore, M.D., John Churchill, London, 1843, p3
[55] Fraser's Magazine, Vol LIV, 1856, London, John W. Parker and Son, Life at the Water Cure, August 1856, pp 197-207

patient was *not* subjected to the toxic mercurial cures so widely in use? Were these cures of ailments, which might all be attributed to nervous degeneration, *not* due to the use of water, but rather to *the absence of use*, and the *elimination by natural means*, of toxic mercurial medications? Consider the following account made by the physician Sir Charles Scudamore:

> *"During my stay at Grafenberg, I heard frequent mention of the stains of mercury and of iodine appearing in the lein-tuchs [wet sheets to lie in], either of blue or reddish color; but Priessnitz assured my friend, Dr. Buxton, that he had seen mercurial globules issue at the ends of the fingers after a continued course of the water cure, in patients who had made a great employment of mercury either internally or externally, or both, notwithstanding that they had desisted from all use of the medicine for even several years! This appears almost incredible. I cannot doubt the veracity of Priessnitz; and Lieberg, with whom I discussed the subject, had no doubt of such a fact, and offered this explanation: that mercury combines with animal matter, and may remain so combined for an indefinite time; and that the quick change of matter which belongs to the water-cure treatment would tend to the separation of the mercury, which might appear in a globular or other form."[56]*

It is difficult to know whether these second hand reports of mercury globules coming out from the skin and staining the treatment sheets of the water-cure patients are fact or myth. If myth, they speak eloquently to the view of an increasing minority, those who believed that mercury as medicine was doing more harm than good. And it is possible that the stories were true. Sweating is, in fact, one of the ways in which the body rids itself of toxic elements such as mercury.[57] As incredible as it seems, it is

---

[56] Ibid, pp 73-74
[57] Arsenic, Cadmium, Lead, and Mercury in Sweat: Margaret E. Sears, Kathleen J. Kerr, Riina I. Bray, J Environ Public Health. V.2012; 2012: 184745

possible that minute amounts of mercury released through sweating by a person who had been highly exposed could have joined together and appeared as drops issuing from the ends of fingers. In addition, there are anecdotal reports by physicians going back many years about mercury coming spontaneously from wounds, as can be seen from this 1762 account by one of the most respected physicians of his day, Richard Mead, physician to King George II:

> *There are many histories of this kind; neither are instances wanting in living persons of Mercury running out of the body, from a tumour, either suppurated, or opened by a caustic: nay there is a case upon record, in which, upon opening a vein, some drachms of it flowed out with the blood.*[58]

Another such report was made in the year 1831, when a physician informed the Westminster Medical Society of a case in which he had applied a blister to the chest of a man with pulmonary consumption, and had given him an ounce of crude mercury internally, only to find, when he later removed the blister that the surface of the skin beneath it "was covered with a multitude of minute globules of metallic mercury." The physicians of the Society were excited by the result, believing that the action of the blister had drawn the medicine "through the seat of the disease."[59] Lieberg's explanation for the phenomenon, "that mercury combines with animal matter," has sound scientific basis. Mercury has a half life of 60 days in the blood, but as it courses through the body it deposits in the tissues of skin and organ and brain and bone, in which it will remain for a much greater period

---

[58] The Medical Works of Richard Mead, M.D., Physician to his late Majesty King George II., London, MDCCLXII, P 107
[59] Murray, J. (1831). *A treatise on pulmonary consumption, its prevention and remedy.* 2d ed. London: Longman, Rees, Orme, Brown, and Green.

of time. There were, in the 1800's, many stories of mercury running from the bodies of the living, in blood and in sweat and from the eruptions of boils and ulcers on the skin. And there were, as well, many stories of mercury found in the bodies of the dead, in the intestines, the lungs, the brain, and the bones, so much so that if the bones of a man who had taken a lot of mercury in life were struck, a fine shower of minute globules of mercury would fly out.[60] This awareness, that mercury could make its way into the bones, formed the basis for an experiment in which French scientist Claude Bernard filled the interior of a dog's femur with quicksilver, closed the perforation with wax, and allowed the wound to heal. Bernard reported that "three months afterwards, most of the metal had disappeared from the bone, but was found in small globules encysted on the surface of the lungs."[61] More recent studies bear this finding out. In November of 2013, two doctors published the case of a man who had injected himself with liquid mercury. An x-ray revealed "innumerable small, high-density opacities diffusely distributed throughout both lungs." It may have begun in the blood, but it wound up in the lungs, causing a multitude of tiny pulmonary emboli.[62]

---

[60] A Treatise on Poisons, by Robert Christison, M.D., 2nd Edition, Longman, Reese, Orme, Brown & Green, London, 1832, pp 352-354

[61] Phillips, C. D. F. (1882). *Materia medica & therapeutics: inorganic substances.* London: J.& A. Churchill., p 624.

[62] *Images in clinical medicine. Pulmonary emboli caused by mercury.* Mamdani H, Vettese TE.,N Engl J Med. 2013 Nov 21;369(21):2031

University Days—Years as an Oxford Professor

*All last autumn and winter my health grew worse and worse:
incessant sickness, tremulous hands, and swimming head. I
thought that I was going the way of all flesh. Having heard of
much success in some cases from the cold-water cure, I
determined to give up all attempts to do anything and come
here and put myself under Dr. Gully.*

-Charles Darwin

In the year 1825, when Charles Dodgson the senior was a young
Oxford mathematics Professor, two men who would have an
enormous impact on British life in the 1800s entered medical
school in Edinburgh—Charles Darwin and James Manby Gully.
Darwin, an uninspired student who had yet to find himself, found
medical school not to his liking, and dropped out after he was
required to attend the autopsy of a child. Gully, however, would
go far. He would become the physician most famous for bringing
Priessnitz's water cure to England, but that is not how he began.
He began his career in the study of neuropathies and neural
degeneration. It was a ripe field of study for an ambitious young
man, as the incidence of neuropathy had been increasing
dramatically for the past 30 years, and was considered with a kind
of distorted pride, to be a disease of civilization, of rich living, of
too much progress, of too much intense effort and thought.

As Gully would write,

*Neuropathy, in any of its degrees, is a disease altogether
unknown among barbarous nations. And there cannot be a
doubt that in all its degrees it has much increased in this country
within the last thirty years, a period in which civilization has
made such giant strides. It is no uncommon thing to hear our*

octogenarian parents say, "That in their youth there were no such things as nerves;"—possibly the cerebral centres of "their youth" were somewhat dull in receiving or making impressions.[63]

One thing was certain, the "cerebral centres" of the Englishmen of Gully's day were not dull in receiving impressions, but on average, *much* more sensitive to stimuli than those of the previous generation. One example of such intensified "nervousness" given by Gully, "In the night-time, the cracking of a piece of furniture, the barking of a dog, or any other common-place noise, caused universal shuddering, and vehement palpitations of the heart. So also, in the streets, the sight of a man, or a horse, though in the distance, if it were approaching him, produced tremors and sinking in the abdomen."[64]

Gully recognized that "the prolonged use of mercurials" could cause neuropathy and nervousness, stating, "Indeed, I feel convinced that seven-tenths of the nervous cases that are met with in this country are the result of excessive medication, which keeps the internal sensibility in a continued state of exaggeration, exciting morbid sympathies, particularly with the brain, until the latter can no longer pass over the visceral sensations." Gully found that by persevering *"in doing next to nothing"* for several months, his patients could find relief from terrible neurological conditions including disordered appetites, nervous over sensibility to stimuli, tingling and numbness of limbs, weakness, nightmarish unrestful sleep, violent headaches, &c.[65] He was primed to become the Water Doctor.

---

[63] An Exposition of the Symptoms, Essential Nature, and Treatment of Neuropathy or Nervousness, by James Manby Gully, London, Churchill, 1837, footnote pp. 76-77
[64] Ibid, p 68
[65] Gully, 1837, p 50

Gully would place the blame for the neuropathic condition of the English on the physician who had advised adoption of American style mercurial therapies, Dr. James Hamilton, the author of the pro-mercury *Observations on the Utility and Administration of Purgative Medicines in Several Diseases*[66] first published in 1805 (and reprinted in at least 6 editions up to 1818), stating sarcastically that "Great should be the reverence of the profession for the name of Hamilton, for many are the interminable cases of neuropathy that owe their origin to his writings!" He found equal fault with John Abernethy, the man who popularized the casual and habitual use of a low dose mercury pill and saline drink combination which would be known as "blue pill and black draught." Gully passionately declared, "if the blue pill and black draught of Abernethy have cleared the tongue of hundreds, I feel convinced that they have also muddled the entire nervous system of thousands."[67]

Abernethy, a surgeon at St. Bartholomew's Hospital in London, was a well-known physician whose book promoting small doses of mercury in the treatment of disease, had been printed in its 8th edition in 1826.[68] (There would be 11 editions in all.) These small doses were typically delivered through pills containing metallic mercury ground together with simple ingredients, such as honey or bread crumb. The pill most favored by the Royal College of Physicians was made as follows:

---

[66] Observations on the Utility and Administration of Purgative Medicines in Several Diseases, by James Hamilton, M.D., 6th Edition, Longman, Hurst, Sees, Orme, and Brown, and T. and G. Underwood, London, 1818
[67] Ibid, pp 106-107
[68] Surgical Observations on the Constitutional Origin and Treatment of Local Diseases, by John Abernethy, 8th edition, London, Longman, Rees, Orme, Brown and Green, 1826.

Two drachms of the mercury are triturated with three drachms of the [red rose] confection, until the globules of the quicksilver have disappeared, and then a drachm of powdered liquorice is added, and the whole mass is beaten until a complete incorporation takes place. . . . Minute division of the mineral is thus effected, and one grain of the mercury is contained in three of the mass. . . .[69]

The pills thus made appeared on physicians prescriptions in Latin as pilulae hydrargyri or pilulae mercuriales, but were known more popularly as "blue pill"—one of the most popular remedies of the day. Abernethy was credited with its popularity, having recommended it repeatedly in his books, to his patients, and also to the many students he taught who would, in the course of their careers, prove loyal followers. His lectures at St. Bartholomew's medical school in London would feature prominently in the very first and many following volumes of the fledgling *Lancet*, a journal designed "to convey to the Public and to distant Practitioners as well as to Students in Medicine and Surgery, reports of the Metropolitan Hospital Lectures."[70]

Abernethy became so associated with blue pill that he would later be believed to have invented it.[71] But, in truth, he had not invented anything, his belief that derangement of the digestive organs was the root of all disease was not new, and neither was the mercury pill. What he excelled at was the ability to inspire the enthusiasm, interest and affection of others. Abernethy's practical and entertaining lectures were so popular that he "generally had a large and attentive class of medical students."[72]

---

[69] Mercury, Blue Pill, and Calomel, by George G. Sigmond, M.D., London, Henry Renshaw, 1840, p44

[70] The Lancet, P1 Vol1, No. 1, London, Sunday, October 5, 1823

[71] "[He has done more harm] than Abernethy with his invention of the blue-pill." The Island, by Richard Whiteing, London, Longmans, Green, And Co., 1888, p170

"On the day of one of his introductory lectures, when the theatre of St. Bartholomew was as full as it could possibly be, and the cheering on his entrance had subsided, he was observed to cast his eyes around, seemingly insensible to the applause with which he had been greeted, and he exclaimed with great feeling and pathos, "God help you all! what is to become of you?" evidently much moved by the appearance of so great a number of medical students, seeking for information to be fitted for practice."[73]

The answer to Abernethy's question is that they would become firm believers, lifelong devotees to Abernethy's stomach-based blue-pill approach to medicine, dosing the English people to within an inch of their lives. They would become a generation of doctors whose careers would have to peak and wane before the world would wake from its mercurial slumber, and forget the dream that had been spun. There was a moment, on waking, that the world remembered, saying such things as, "Blue pill was the fashion, blue pill the scourge of our predecessors,"[74] but quickly the memory would fade away. "What an amount of mercury, in the form of blue pill, has been given to the generation now passing away!" would write one man in the year 1898, the year Charles Dodgson's son, not yet born, would die.[75] But we are getting ahead of ourselves.

---

[72]Physic and Physicians: a Medical Sketch Book, Exhibiting the Public and Private Life of the Most Celebrated Medical Men, Vol I, Part I, London, Longman, Orme, Brown, and Co. 1839, p 111.

[73] Ibid, p 119

[74] The Story of Thomas Carlyle, by A. S. Arnold, London, Ward and Downey, 1888, pp 215-216

[75] An Old English Home and its Dependencies, by Sabine Baring-Gould (1834-1924), London, Methuen & Co. 1898, p 254

Country Life—a Son is Born

He confirms an observation of mine, which indeed I find is hundreds of years old, that a stammering man is never a worthless one. Physiology can tell you why. It is an excess of delicacy, excess of sensibility to the presence of his fellow creature, that makes him stammer.

-Thomas Carlyle

In 1827, Charles Dodgson the senior married, and by doing so, was required to give up his professorship at Oxford. He was appointed to a "living" at All Saints Church in Daresbury. Clergymen had traditionally been provided with such a "benefice," a property intended to produce revenue to support their needs. When Elizabeth I became Queen of England in 1558, one of her first acts was to command the beneficed clergy to contribute a certain proportion of their revenues to the education of poor scholars "to the intent that learned men may hereafter spring the more." Had Charles Dodgson, the son of a well-positioned clergyman, been by nepotism, the recipient of aid that had originally been intended for the education and elevation of the talented poor? If he was, he certainly wasn't alone. The clergy were allowed to *choose* their "poor scholars," and had, before they were allowed to marry, given their preference to the children of family and friends. When, therefore, they were later allowed to marry and had children of their own, it was considered "no less decent and natural in them to prefer their own children before all other applicants for help." The transfer of this charitable support from members of the congregation to the offspring of clerical parents was supported by interpreting the ultimate purpose of Elizabeth I's injunction to be "the supply of a sufficient number of persons competent to discharge the functions of the priesthood." This loss of financial aid for the education of the poor was considered to be more than compensated for by the increase in persons qualified to minister to the spiritual needs of the community.[76]

However he had arrived at his position, Dodgson took it seriously and devoted himself to the health and spiritual welfare of his parishioners, opening a charity school with his wife's help, and ministering to barge workers who passed through the town on the Bridgewater canal which led to Runcorn. Frances Jane Lutwidge Dodgson, as the wife of a country clergyman, also had an important role in the life of the Daresbury parish. While the reverends were caring for the spiritual health of their congregations, their wives cared for the physical health, ministering to the needs of the ill, the poor, and the hungry.

As late as 1816, English law did not require that medical practitioners in country districts have education beyond an apprenticeship to an apothecary. Some of the doctors who had begun their practice before the change in law returned to school to obtain their medical certificates, but most did not, choosing instead to buy fake German or Scotch diplomas and to continue in practice. [77] It is not surprising, then, that the country doctors tended to rely heavily on books such as Hamilton's and Abernethy's which reduced all complaints to the need for a mercurial purgative. Fletcher Moss , a writer specializing in humorous looks at life in the nearby parsonage of Didsbury, Cheshire, would write the following account of a village doctor

---

[76] A Book About the Clergy, John Cordy Jeaffreson, Vol 1, London, Hurst and Blackett, Publishers, 1870, pp 315-320

[77] A Book about Doctors, J. Cordy Jeaffreson, Vol II, London, Hurst and Blackett, Publishers, 1860 pp 276-277

sent for to attend to a French governess who became ill while in service at the Cheadle seminary.

> *The village doctor was sent for, and his practice was simplicity itself, for he had one question and one cure for all cases. He asked his question, which sounded like "Howsthbowls?" and the new governess did not understand a word of English, though it might not have made any difference if she had understood him, for she got the universal cure, the calomel pill, locally called a white bulldog. The next day she was worse, and could only feebly moan, "Non, m'sieur, non" but she had to take another white bulldog.* [78]

The relative ignorance of the country doctors, and the pride of an educated clergy, made a situation ripe for exploitation, and a series of medical advice books aimed at clergymen and heads of families began to be published. These books were ostensibly designed for country folk living in areas where professional medical advice could not be quickly obtained, and as a rule, they recommended obtaining medical help, then provided an encyclopedic summary of various illnesses along with the medications useful in treating those illnesses, among which figured prominently, mercurial ointments, blue pill and calomel. Charles Dodgson the senior, having just entered the clergy, and appointed to a sleepy country parish, would have been the target audience.

In one such book, *Medical Hints Designed for the Use of Clergymen* published in 1829, the author/physician, Henry Bickersteth, recommended mercurial medications in a wide range of illnesses; as an alterative, as a purgative, for watering eyes, for eczema, for croup (inflammation of the windpipe), for typhus and rheumatic fever, rheumatism, for jaundice and inflammation of

---

[78] Moss, F. (1898). *Folk-lore, old customs and tales of my neighbours.* .

the liver, for paralysis and St. Vitus's Dance or Chorea ("convulsions in which the arms and legs are thrown about"). Bickersteth had such a pro-mercury stance that he went so far as to include a recommendation for mercury as the usual treatment in hydrocephalus, although he had "never yet seen this to succeed," rationalizing that despite the fact that mercury had little chance of success in hydrocephalus, "it should certainly be given so as to keep the chylopoetic viscera in order." (Chylopoetic refers to the function of the liver in secreting chyle, or bile.)[79] Some of the specifics recommended by Bickersteth; for croup in children, calomel given every hour, until the breathing is relieved, For convulsions in children and young persons up to 14, three grains of calomel every, or every other morning, for watery eyes, 1/3 of a grain of blue pill taken 3 or 4 times a day, as well as an ointment containing white precipitated mercury every night before bed, for eczema, mercurial ointment, or, if a stubborn case, Plummer's Pills (a mixture of calomel and antimony) to be taken morning and night, as an alterative, half a grain to two grains of calomel every night, and as a purgative for an adult, five to fifteen grains of calomel.[80]

Thomas Ayre Bromhead dedicated his book *The Parents Medical and Surgical Assistant* to the Magistrates, Parochial Clergy, and Country Gentlemen of Great Britain, writing, "This work, intended as a guide to direct their humane efforts in the palliation of suffering, and preservation of life, under circumstances of urgent and imperious necessity." Bromhead explained that his recommendations might not be that which a physician would necessarily issue, *if they were present*, but rather, "the means most accessible to the unprepared and uninformed,

[79] Medical Hints, designed for the use of Clergymen, by Henry Bickersteth, 3rd Edition, London, R.B. Seeley and W. Burnside, 1829
[80] Ibid, pp 29-30, 32, 49, 63, 68, 73, 77, 108, 124

most easy and simple of application." Bromhead's book said straight out what the other books merely implied, that certain medicines, including calomel, "should be kept by every family residing in a district remote from Medical Assistance." Calomel, wrote Bromhead, was of "great use" in the case of croup, and he recommended that it be given "—to an infant of six months, a *grain and a half* every hour until it purge freely; to a child a year old, *two grains*; and to one of two years, *three or four grains* may be given every hour until the bowels are freely acted upon..."[81]

More such books would follow, such as Fenwick Skrimshire's *Village Pastor's Surgical and Medical Guide*, outlining the ways in which conscientious country reverends could fulfill their duties in aiding their parishioners in the absence of a qualified medical practitioner, advising, among other things, full doses of calomel for fevers accompanied by vomiting and diarrhea, and, in the case of protracted intermittent fever, advising that the patient be left with half a dozen or more five-grain blue pills, with directions to take one every 4th night. [82] Similar medical advice books in the United States were even more to the point, such as this advice printed in *The Western Journal of the Medical and Physical Sciences* in 1834, and reprinted in *Regimen and Simple Medicines* (1838) on the treatment of cholera,

> *The treatment by calomel alone, is so very simple, that I should hereafter say to the public: Have an ounce of calomel in every house, made up into ten grain pills."*[83]

---

[81] The Parents Medical and Surgical Assistant, by Thomas Ayre Bromhead, London, Harvey and Darton, 1830

[82] The Village pastor's surgical and medical guide: in letters from an old physician to a young clergymen, his son, on his entering upon the duties of a parish priest, by Fenwick Skrimshire, M.D., London, John Churchill, 1838, p 234

[83] The Western Journal of the Medical and Physical Sciences, edited by Daniel Drake, M.D., Vol. VII, The Chronicle Office, Cincinnati, Ohio, 1834, p 332; Domestic Medicine, A Treatise on the Prevention and Cure of Diseases by

It was into *this* world that Charles Lutwidge Dodgson was born. Charles would be one of 11 children, and he, his brother Edwin, and almost all of his sisters would have a stammer, or hesitation of speech. Because Charles Dodgson and his wife Fanny (the former Frances Jane Lutwidge) were first cousins, most Lewis Carroll biographers have presumed a genetic basis to the stammering—the only explanation which they believed could explain such an anomalous clustering of stammering in a single family—but they have overstated their case. Current medical research has confirmed that genetics *do* play a part in the *manifestation* of stammering, but the degree of heritability they have found is too weak to explain the prevalence of stammering in the Dodgson family. Sibling studies have found the concordance of stammering in identical twins to be 1 in 11, meaning that if 1 in a set of identical twins stammers, the likelihood that the other twin will also stammer is 1 in 11, a decided increase over the rate of concordance in non-twin siblings of 1 in 35.[84] The Dodgson siblings, as children of two first cousins, would lie somewhere in between the twin and non-twin categories, with less genes in common than identical twins, but more genes in common than non-twin siblings from unrelated parents. Here, the incredible coincidence that there is a 1 in 11 stammering concordance between identical twins, individuals who by definition *both* have the gene predisposing them to stammer, and the fact that there were *11* Dodgson children serves to disprove genetics as the cause of the stammering. Past biographers have overlooked the fact that hesitations and other defects in speech are *known* to occur as a result of neural

Regimen and Simple Medicines, by William Buchan, M.D. , U.P. James, Cincinnati, 1838, p 287

[84]Kraft SJ, Yairi E, Genetic bases of stuttering: the state of the art, 2011, Folia Phoniatr Logop. 2012;64(1):34-47

degeneration brought about by *external* factors, such as, and including, mercury exposure.

In the 1800s it was believed, and it is in fact true, that children's immature nervous systems are more easily excited and derailed than that of an adult. They also believed, *falsely*, that bowel complaints led to nervous derangement *and* that mercury could be used to increase biliary secretions and improve digestion. Their wayward conclusion was that it was critically important to treat children exhibiting signs of disordered digestion with mercury. Compounding their false logic was the unfortunate fact that children do not salivate in response to mercury exposure as readily as adults, causing physicians of the time to state that children could tolerate *larger* doses of mercury than an adult could handle without ill effect. It was therefore not uncommon to administer mercurial purges in the first month of life, using small doses of mercury dissolved in breast milk. Unfortunately, if this treatment caused intestinal distress, it was likely that the people of the time would interpret the symptoms as an indication that the smaller dose had been insufficient, and that a larger dose should be employed, as much as 10 grains of calomel.

"It is not unfrequently proper during the first month to administer mercurial purges. The Blue Pill (No. 7), in the dose of one or two dissolved in a teaspoonful of breast-milk, is generally sufficient. Should this not act sufficiently, Calomel (no. 3) In the dose of four to eight grains, should be administered. There is no danger of salivating young children. Owing to the mucus or slimy matter of the bowels, children will often require as large a dose of calomel as adults. When convulsions are present, the warm bath should be used with cathartics in full doses.[85]

---

[85] Ritter, Thomas (1896) A Medical Manual And Medicine Chest Companion, New York: Trow Directory, Printing and Bookbinding Co., pp 92-93

Unfortunately for children of the time, teething was also believed to cause irritation of the bowels. It is much more likely that upsets in digestion were brought about by the introduction of the child's first solid foods, but because the effects of disordered digestion were believed to pose a hazard to the child's developing nervous system, a compound soda comprised of mercury, soda and chalk was often prescribed as a mild purgative during the teething period.[86] Mercury in teething powders would have serious and often fatal consequences for the children exposed to them, but this was not known to be the case until the mid-1900s. Until that time, mercurial teething powders were believed to be benign and they did not require a doctor's prescription to obtain. Any concerned and proactive mother could go to the chemist and have some powders mixed up. All of this mercury was, of course, in addition to any that might be employed by physicians during the course of childhood illnesses.

We cannot know whether the Dodgson children were *in fact* treated with mercury in the absence of a written record of the fact, even if we can say that it is *extremely likely* that they were. It is much easier to begin researching mercury and to find those with recorded exposure, than it is in the converse, to begin with an individual and to then find mercury exposure. But we do know that Charles Dodgson's hesitation of speech, and the partial deafness he had in one ear, began after a fever he had as a child, and that his deafness increased and became permanent after treatment for mumps as a boy.[87]

---

[86] Inquire Within for Anything you Want to Know, or Over Three Thousand Seven Hundred Facts Worth Knowing, New York: Dick & Fitzgerald (1858), p 161

[87] In a letter from Mrs. Dodgson to her sister Lucy Lutwidge, "With regard to dearest Charlie I hope to have heard from him again today, but I have not. In his letter received on Tuesday he says that the mumps had gone but that they had left him much more deaf than usual—this we trust is quite to be accounted

When Charles grew up, he would spend his life trying to introduce children to greater questions of logic, mathematics and science, in such a way that they did not know they were being taught, and he expressed his desire to conceal these questions in each amusing knot-like puzzle "like the medicine so dexterously, but ineffectually, concealed in the jam of our early childhood."[88] What was the medicine *he* was given? We will never know, but we do know that calomel was often given in jam or bread, and that mercury pills were often made easier to swallow by giving them in bread or jelly.[89]

---

for from the nature of the complaint and may probably last longer than the visible swelling of the glands. Charles has however written to Dr. Tait telling him of Charlie's former deafness & its source (Infantile fever) & requesting him to take the best medical opinion within his reach & to report it immediately to us." The Diaries of Lewis Carroll, edited by Roger Lancelyn Green, 1954, vol 1, p 19,

[88] A Tangled Tale, by Lewis Carroll, London: Macmillan and Co. 1886, preface

[89] The library of home economics; a complete home-study v. 9 Chicago: American School of Home Economics 1907 Home care of the sick, by Amy Elizabeth Pope, p 50

Part II

Lewis Carroll and the Ambiguous Middle

The Illogic of Dreams

When we will admit undefinable and unconscious premises and assertions, any madman may argue us into convictions of utter absurdity.

-George Field,
The Analogy of Logic and Logic of Analogy

On the 4th of July in 1862, 30 year old Oxford mathematics professor Charles Lutwidge Dodgson rowed down a tributary of the river Thames towards Godstow with his friend Robinson Duckworth, and the three young daughters of the Dean of Christ Church college, Lorina, Alice, and Edith Liddell. It was a hot day, and the little group landed their boat on the banks of a grassy meadow and relaxed in the shade of a tall haystack. The girls pushed around Dodgson and eagerly asked him to tell them a story. He began, at their urging, to tell the story of a girl named Alice who was falling asleep while sitting next to her sister on a river bank, when a white rabbit wearing a waist coat and carrying a pocket watch suddenly ran close by her, and how she, burning with curiosity, followed it down its rabbit hole, falling, falling, falling into the dream of Wonderland.

Dodgson told the story the way you tell stories to children, incorporating all of the little details of their everyday lives to make it personal and get their attention—a girl named Alice, sisters sitting on the bank of a meadow, the girls' cat Dinah, a perfect sunny summer day. And then—to make it exciting— fantastical creatures, talking rabbits, mock turtles, "a Duck and a Dodo, a Lory and an Eaglet, and several other curious creatures."[90]

Carroll biographers have told us that beside Alice herself, the Dodo, the Duck, the Lory and the Eaglet represented those present when Dodgson began telling his fairy tale, Dodgson himself, Robinson Duckworth, Lorina and Edith Liddell.

Robinson Duckworth confirmed that this was so in a letter written to Dodgson's nephew and biography Stuart Dodgson Collingwood after Dodgson's death,

Five-and-thirty years ago, when I was an Oxford tutor, I received frequent notes from the Rev. C. L. Dodgson, but I am afraid that these have all been destroyed, and since I left Oxford in 1866 I have seldom had communication with him.

I was very closely associated with him in the production and publication of 'Alice in Wonderland.' I rowed stroke and he rowed bow in the famous Long Vacation voyage to Godstow, when the three Miss Liddells were our passengers, and the story was actually composed and spoken over my shoulder for the benefit of Alice Liddell, who was acting as 'cox' of our gig. I remember turning round and saying, Dodgson, is this an extempore romance of yours?' And he replied, 'Yes, I'm inventing as we go along.' I also well remember how, when we had conducted the three children back to the Deanery, Alice said, as she bade us good-night, 'Oh Mr. Dodgson, I wish you would write out Alice's adventures for me.' He said he should try, and he afterwards told me that he sat up nearly the whole night, committing to a M.S. book his recollections of the drolleries with which he had enlivened the afternoon. He added illustrations of his own, and presented the volume, which used often to be seen on the drawing-room table at the Deanery.

One day Henry Kingsley, when on a visit to the Dean, took up the M.S., and read it through with the greatest delight, urging Mrs. Liddell to persuade the author to publish it.[91]

[90] Carroll, L, (1865) *Alice's Adventures In Wonderland.* New York: H.M. Caldwell co., p 35

[91] Carroll, L. (1899). *The Lewis Carroll picture book: a selection from the*

Dodgson had been writing poetry, essays and stories for years, and he had successfully submitted several pieces for publication in various magazines, such as *The Whitby Gazette*, *The Oxonian Advertiser*, *College Rhymes*, and *The Train*, but he had not thought of publishing *Alice* before this point.[92] You could make a little money publishing poetry and other short pieces in magazines, but authors in the 1800s were responsible for a significant portion of the upfront costs incurred in publishing their books. Dodgson showed Alice around, and he received such a favorable response that he decided to go ahead with publication, but before he did, he set about revising the story.

Dodgson had written the first Alice, *Alice's Adventures Underground*, as a wild adventure that was revealed to be a dream when the attack of a living deck of cards became the flurry of leaves which blew into Alice's face and awakened her. It was a story which incorporated Dodgson's long term interest in abnormal states of consciousness. He had been musing on the subject as far back as 1856, years before he began Alice, when he wrote in his diary,

> *Feb 9. (Sat). Query: when we are dreaming and, as often happens, have a dim consciousness of the fact and try to wake, do we not say and do things which in waking life would be insane? May we not then sometimes define insanity as an inability to distinguish which is the waking and which the sleeping life? We often dream without the least suspicion of unreality: "Sleep hath its own world", and it is often as lifelike as the other.*

---

unpublished writings and drawings of Lewis Carroll : together with reprints from scarce and unacknowledged work. London: T.F. Unwin., Lewis Carroll Picture Book, pp 358-360
[92] Ibid., p 17

The nature of insanity was a natural focus of mind for Dodgson, whose favorite uncle, Skeffington Lutwidge, was a lunacy commissioner—one of a small group of men tasked with overseeing the various lunatic asylums throughout the country. Some men, having seen the lesions and shrunken areas of the brains of the autopsied insane, blamed cerebral disease and neural degeneration for insanity, but most men explored metaphysical explanations, such as errors in perception, thought and logic. The man who thinks he is made of glass, they would say, isn't wrong to think that he shouldn't knock himself against the wall, the error is in the original assumption. If you could work through the puzzle of the lunatics thought processes, and help him to see past his emotions and to understand where he was in error, his thought processes would correct themselves. Those who believed that insanity was an error in thought processes believed that men with well trained and logical minds rarely suffered insanity, although others, quite famously said that all men were mad. And you couldn't fault their logic. If errors in thought processes and morality defined insanity, it was undeniable that all men could be defined as mad to some degree.[93]

When Dodgson revised Alice, increasing the story from 12,715 words, to 26,708 words, he *reduced* the primacy of the original party, and removed a soliloquy by Alice which too closely identified the characters ("really the Lory and I were almost like sisters! and so was that dear little Eaglet! And then the Duck and the Dodo! How nicely the Duck sang to us as we came along through the water; and if the Dodo hadn't known the way to that

---

[93] Johnson, H. James., Johnson, J. *The Medico-chirurgical review.* [London: S. Highley] Vol 17 (1830), p 93; Arnold, T. (1806). *Observations on the nature, kinds, causes, and prevention of insanity.* 2d ed., cor. and improved ... London: R. Phillips., p 66; Slack, R. (1856). *Old truths and modern progress.* London: Hamilton, Adams and Co., p 130; Clouston, T. S. 1840-1915. (1911). *Unsoundness of mind.* London: Methuen & co., ltd., p 320

nice little cottage, I don't know when we should have got dry again—"[94]).   Mindful that he was an Oxford mathematics professor, and wanting to maintain the dignity of that position, Dodgson wrote the revised book under the pseudonym Lewis Carroll, a name which he had fashioned a few years before out of Charles Lutwidge by translating it into Latin to produce Carolus Ludovicus, and then translating Carolus Ludovicus back into English to produce Carroll Lewis, and then reversing Carroll Lewis to produce Lewis Carroll.

As Lewis Carroll, he *added* the Cheshire cat, the March hare, and the Hatter, none of which had been present in the original story and all of whom serve to introduce a heightened sense of madness.   The Cheshire cat[95] introduces himself to Alice as mad, and then launches into a form of logical argument known as a syllogism to prove the fact.   Using the example of a dog as a creature which they could both agree was *not* mad, the cat then states, "a dog growls when it's angry, and wags its tail when it's pleased.   Now *I* growl when I'm pleased, and wag my tail when I'm angry.   Therefore I'm mad."   A syllogism is a form of logical argument in which two premises, or statements of fact, are used to prove a conclusion, or, as Carroll would put it later; a "sillygism" is a logical argument in which two premises are used to produce a *delusion*.[96]   In this case, the "delusion" is produced by the use of ambiguous words in the middle term of the argument,

---

[94] Carroll, L. (1886) Alice's Adventures Under Ground, Being a Facsimile of the Original MS. Book, London: Macmillan and Co.

[95] Some believe that the Cheshire cat's habit of disappearing slowly, tail first, grin last, is, a reference, some say, to wheels of Cheshire Cheese made in the shape of the grinning cats the county of Cheshire was famous for, a cheese which would be eaten from the outside in, leaving the grin as last. Dodgson would have been familiar with both the saying and the cheese, as he was born and lived the first eleven years of his life in Cheshire.

[96] Carroll, L. (1889). *Sylvie and Bruno*. London: Macmillan, p 259.

such as growl for purr. Alice is not taken in, and replies, "I call it purring, not growling."

This form of logical fallacy is called a fallacy of the ambiguous middle, and it arises from the use of language that lends itself to more than one interpretation. A clear example of an ambiguous middle would be—*seven is one number; five and two are seven; therefore five and two are one number*. The premise, seven is one number is a given; but the *ambiguous* use in the middle term of the word "are" (a word often used in spoken equations to mean "equals") leads to a false conclusion. Logicians, attempting to identify the ambiguities of complex arguments, reduce verbal phrases into what seems a dizzying *increase* in complexity to the ordinary mind. An example of this can be found in the Duchess's simplification of the phrase "Be what you would seem to be" found in *Alice's Adventures in Wonderland*, when the Duchess simplifies the statement, " Be what you would seem to be " as follows:

> *Never imagine yourself / not to be otherwise / than what it might / appear to others / that what you were / or might have been / was not otherwise / than what you had been / would have appeared to them / to be otherwise.*

The identification of this phrase as utilizing symbolic logic and the demarcations of its component parts were made by the logician and Nobel Laureate Bertrand Russell, who states that logical simplicity can very often only be obtained by apparently complicated statements because of the subtle psychological implications ordinary language frequently contains. [97] (That

---

[97] Jourdain, P. E. B. 1879-1919. (1918). *The philosophy of Mr. B*rtr*nd R*ss**ll: with an appendix of leading passages from certain other works*. London: G. Allen & Unwin., p 91. The clumsy attempt at identifying and separating out the propositions with "/" marks is my own.

Russell was correct in his identification is more than confirmed by Carroll's later work, *The Game of Logic*, in which he tried to educate young children about symbolic logic by breaking down phrases through the use of counters and diagrams.) However, while mathematicians and logicians might see this and other statements from the Alice books as illustrative of various forms of logical arguments, they were accepted by the general public as high nonsense and little more.

And they loved the fact that it meant nothing. *The Harvard Advocate* wrote, "it is a great relief, now and then, to come across a laughing little Puck among books, like this, which seems to have come into existence with no other idea than fun, pure and simple." [98] They loved that it was both simple and cunning and filled with "bewilderingly stupid animals" that would nevertheless argue with Alice and call her out on her mistakes.[99] They loved Carroll's "world of strange wonders" and the way it was a "near echo" of the familiar. Funnily enough, when they complained, it was about the parts in which the book appeared to veer too close to "direct" satire.[100] The truth of the matter was they didn't *want* it to mean anything. And if you don't either—it may be time to stop reading.

---

[98] *The Harvard Advocate*. Vol VII (1869) Cambridge, Mass: Harvard University, p 108

[99] *The New eclectic magazine*. Vol 5 (1869) Baltimore, Md.: Turnbull & Murdoch., pp 231-232

[100] *The contemporary review*. Vol 11 (1869) London: A. Strahan, pp. 24-25

Tea Time

In Alice's Adventures in Wonderland, when Alice arrives at the March Hare's house, with its chimneys shaped like ears, and its fur thatched roof, she finds a table set out under a tree in front of the house, and the March Hare and the Hatter sitting at it having tea, with a Dormouse sitting between them, fast asleep. It is quite a large table, with many place settings, but the three of them are crowded together at one corner of it. You see, it is always 6 o'clock, tea time, so those at the party don't have the time to clean up, but must simply move on to the next place setting when they have used up what is before them. Alice sits down at the table, and after a smattering of odd conversation, the Hatter suddenly asks Alice, *"Why is a raven like a writing-desk?"* While she is still trying to figure the answer, the Hatter asks her, *"What day of the month is it?"* When she responds that it is the fourth, he sighs and says that his watch is two days wrong. It is a "funny" watch, Alice remarks, noting that it marks time *not* by the hours of the day in the way that a usual watch does, but by the days of the month.

An excerpt from the tea party is as follows:

"Why should it?" muttered the Hatter. "Does *your* watch tell you what year it is?"
"Of course not," Alice replied very readily; "but that's because it stays the same year for such a long time together."
"Which is just the case with *mine*," said the Hatter.

Alice felt dreadfully puzzled. The Hatter's remark seemed to her to have no sort of meaning in it, and yet it was certainly English. "I don't quite understand you," she said as politely as she could.

"The Dormouse is asleep again," said the Hatter, and he poured a little hot tea onto its nose.

The Dormouse shook its head impatiently, and said, without opening its eyes, "Of course, of course; just what I was going to remark myself."

"Have you guessed the riddle yet?" the Hatter said, turning to Alice again.

"No; I give it up," Alice replied: "what's the answer?"

"I haven't the slightest idea," said the Hatter.

"Nor I," said the March Hare.

Alice sighed wearily. "I think you might do something better with the time," she said, "than wasting it in asking riddles that have no answers."

"If you knew Time as well as I do," said the Hatter, "you wouldn't talk about wasting *it*. It's *him*."

"I don't know what you mean," said Alice.

"Of course you don't!" the Hatter said, tossing his head contemptuously. "I dare say you never even spoke to Time!"

"Perhaps not," Alice cautiously replied; "but I know I have to beat time when I learn music."

"Ah! that accounts for it," said the Hatter. "He won't stand beating. Now, if you only kept on good terms with him, he'd do almost anything you liked with the clock. For instance, suppose it were nine o'clock in the morning, just time to begin lessons: you'd only have to whisper a hint to Time, and round goes the clock in a twinkling! Half-past-one, time for dinner!"

("I only wish it was," the March Hare said to itself in a whisper.)

"That would be grand, certainly," said Alice thoughtfully; "but then—I shouldn't be hungry for it, you know."

"Not at first, perhaps," said the Hatter, "but you could keep it to half-past one as long as you liked."

"Is that the way you manage?" Alice asked.

The Hatter shook his head mournfully. "Not I," he replied. "We quarreled last March—just before *he* went mad, you know" (pointing with his teaspoon at the March Hare); "It was at the great concert given by the Queen of Hearts, and I had to sing:—

"'Twinkle, twinkle, little bat!

How I wonder what you're at!'
You know the song perhaps?"
"I've heard something like it," said Alice.
"It goes on, you know," the Hatter continued, "in this way:—
    '"Up above the world you fly,
    Like a tea-tray in the sky.
       Twinkle, twinkle'"—
Here the Dormouse shook itself, and began singing in its sleep, ""Twinkle, twinkle, twinkle"—and went on for so long that they had to pinch it to make it stop.
"Well, I'd hardly finished the first verse," said the Hatter, "when the Queen bawled out 'He's murdering the time! Off with his head!'"
"How dreadfully savage!" exclaimed Alice.
"And ever since that," the Hatter went on in a mournful tone, "he won't do a thing I ask! It's always six o'clock now."

The Hatter had a special relationship with time, he was able to cause it to move or stop on a whim, at least before he "murdered" it. Murdering time was a common play on words in Lewis Carroll's time, a simple joke playing off of a double meaning in conjunction with keeping a beat, or beating time, to keep the rhythm in a musical performance, as can be seen from the following passage in the 1826 *Punster's Pocket-book*,

When Kemble was rehearsing the romance sung by Richard Coeur de Lion, Shaw, the leader of the band, called out from the orchestra, "Mr. Kemble, my dear Mr. Kemble, you are murdering time." Kemble, calmly and cooly taking a pinch of snuff, said, "My dear Sir, it is better for me to murder Time at once than be continually beating him as you do."[101]

Notice that Kemble casually refers to time as "him", personifying time in the same way the Hatter does. The more

---

[101] Westmacott, C. M. 1787 or 8-1868. (1826). *The punster's pocket-book.* Lond. P 116.

familiar you become with the literature of the time, the more references like this you can find that precede and suggest Lewis Carroll's work. It is as if Carroll used *everything* he had been exposed to, and churned it up and mixed it together, his special genius being a reinterpretation of adult complexities for the amusement of children. In this case, a child's eye view of what would happen if you *literally* murdered time.

Remember that it is always 6 o'clock and time for tea for the Hatter, so that when he is called as the first witness in the trial of the Knave of Hearts (which occurs later in the book), he comes in with a teacup in one hand, and a piece of bread and butter in the other. When he *began* his tea becomes a subject of questioning, and one which yields 3 different answers—the Hatter thinks it was the fourteenth of March, the March Hare estimates the Fifteenth, and the Dormouse, the Sixteenth. The King then directs the jury to "write that down," at which point the jury writes down the figures, adds them up, and reduces the answer to shillings and pence. A reference to the saying, which is much older than you might suppose, that "time is money?" It was, in fact, an old concept which was popularized by Benjamin Franklin in his essay, *Advice to a Young Tradesman*, which was reprinted exactly as follows many, many times in England, from the late 1700's until the publication of *Alice's Adventures*, and beyond: "Remember that time is money. He that can earn 10 shillings a day by his labour, and goes abroad, or sits idle one half of that day, though he spend but 6 pence during his diversion or idleness, ought not to reckon that the only expense; he has really spent, or rather thrown away, 5 shillings besides."[102] Is this, then, the origin of the

---

[102] A few in example showing the pervasiveness of the quotation—Franklin, B. (1793). *Works of the late Doctor Benjamin Franklin:: consisting of his life, written by himself; together with essays, humorous, moral & literary, chiefly in the manner of the Spectator.* Dublin:: Printed for P. Wogan, P. Byrne, J. Moore,

10/6, ten shillings, six pence price tag on the hatter's hat? That time can be spent wisely, or it can be wasted?

Whatever the finer points, there is an infatuation with time here, obvious to even the most superficial inspection. That characterization is carried forward in the 2nd *Alice* Book, *Through the Looking Glass*, in which the characters are living *backwards* in time, so that the Hatter (now referred to in corrupted dialect as Hatta)[103], is in prison at the beginning of the book, being punished, with the trial beginning later, and the crime coming last of all (in the earlier book, in fact). When Hatta enters the story, he is standing with a cup of tea in one hand, and a piece of bread-and-butter in the other. "He's only just out of prison, and he hadn't finished his tea when he was sent in," Haigha (pronounced to rhyme with 'mayor') explains. The characterization of the Hatter and March Hare as King's Messengers is an exceptionally clever reference to Adams 1849 allegory, *the King's Messengers*[104], in which the image of the past appears in a mirror held up before a dying man, showing visions of the needy poor, the "King's Messengers" whom he had helped in life. It was a story which emphasized that *God-given time is the real treasure*, a message

---

and W. Jones.. Advice to a Young Tradesman, Written Anno 1748, p. 188; (1821). *A father's gift to his son, on his becoming an apprentice: to which is added Dr. Franklin's Way to wealth.* New York: Wood.., p 12. Mavor, W. Fordyce. (1825). *The English spelling-book: accompanied by a progressive series of easy and familiar lessons, intended as an introduction to the reading and spelling of the English language.* 306. ed., rev. London: Longman, Hurst, Rees, Orme, Brown and Green., p 106, Advice to Young Persons Intended for Trade, by Dr. Benjamin Franklin; Timbs, J. (1856). *Laconics, or The best words of the best authors.* 8th ed. London: H.S. Bohn., p 230

103 The Hatter and the March Hare reappear in Through the Looking Glass as the King's Messengers, Hatta and Haigha (pronounced to rhyme with 'mayor'.).

104 Adams, W. (1849). *Sacred allegories: The shadow of the cross, The distant hills, The old man's home, the King's Messengers.* London: F.&J. Rivington., Kingsley's Alton Locke, and Carlyle's French Revolution.

which Carroll, as a member of the clergy would repeat in later works of fiction, somewhat more clearly than he has here.

Because the Hatter is so obviously obsessed with time, many *Alice* historians have seconded a theory put forward years ago that the Hatter was based on an eccentric furniture maker named Theophilus Carter who lived in Oxford, who always wore a tall hat, and who had supposedly, although this has not been proven, invented a clever alarm clock which would tip the user out of bed in the morning—a sort of Wallace and Grommit style of invention. In order to second this theory, historians have had to ignore a clue passed on by Carroll's nephew, Stuart Dodgson Collingwood,—that the Hatter was indeed based on a real person, and *that* person had been in Lewis Carroll's dining group at Oxford—a clue that excluded the Oxford furniture maker. "In those days," wrote his nephew, "the undergraduates dining in hall were divided into "messes." Each mess consisted of about half a dozen men, who had a table to themselves. . . . In Mr. Dodgson's mess were Philip Pusey, the late Rev. G. C. Woodhouse, and, among others, one who still lives in "Alice in Wonderland" as the "Hatter."[105]

There was, of course, one obvious person whom Collingwood's clue included, a man "who still lives in Alice and Wonderland", and who ate at Lewis Carroll's dining table, a man who always wore a top hat even at the seaside, even in shirt sleeves and in the warmest weather, a man given to nonsense

---

[105] Present at Carroll's table were Apsley Cherry, Charles John Hampden (the son of the Bishop of Hereford), Philip Edward Pusey (the son of Edward Bouverie Pusey), and George Gridlestone Woodhouse. "In those days the undergraduates dining in hall were divided into "messes." Each mess consisted of about half a dozen men, who had a table to themselves. . . . In Mr. Dodgson's mess were Philip Pusey, the late Rev. G. C. Woodhouse, and, among others, one who still lives in "Alice in Wonderland" as the "Hatter." Collingwood, S. Dodgson. (1899). *The life and letters of Lewis Carroll (Rev. C.L. Dodgson)*. New York: The Century Co.. p. 47; Wakeling, E. (2001) Lewis Carroll's Diaries, The Private Journals of Charles Lutwidge Dodgson, Vol. 10, pp 400-402

and obsessed with time, and that was Lewis Carroll himself.[106] This form of "he was there with me" riddle was commonly used by Carroll, and it wasn't meant to be difficult to puzzle out. Note, for example, this excerpt of a letter written in 1869 by Dodgson to a young girl,

> *A friend of mine, called Mr. Lewis Carroll, tells me he means to send you a book. He is a very dear friend of mine. I have known him all my life—we are the same age—and have never left him. Of course he was with me in the Gardens, not a yard off—even while I was drawing those puzzles for you. I wonder if you saw him?[107]*

Not only is this a typical form of teasing Dodgson indulged in (not a yard off, a misleading but literal truth), if you look at the questions about time posed by the Hatter, you will see that they have many elements in common with two logical conundrums about time which Dodgson was known to pose so repeatedly to those around him that he was said to have ruined many a good dinner party with the puzzles.[108]

Charles Dodgson was born into a world before standardized time, a world in which each small town kept its own local time based on the midday position of the sun. This posed little difficulty until the introduction of the railroad, at which time the lack of a standardized time was found to cause nightmarish difficulties in scheduling railway arrival and departure times.[109] In

---

[106] "He always wore a top hat, even when boating or at the seashore" and yet "He hardly ever wore an overcoat, no matter what the state of the weather might be." The Lantern, edited by Theodore F. Bonnet and Edward F. O'Day, Vol. 3, December 1917 No. 9, The Father of Alice, by Edward F. O'Day, p 21

[107] Cook, A. S. 1853-1927. (1905). *Specimen letters*. Boston: Ginn, p 105.

[108] "The difficulty of answering this apparently simple question has cast a gloom over many a pleasant party." Collingwood, S. Dodgson. (1899). *The life and letters of Lewis Carroll (Rev. C.L. Dodgson)*. New York: The Century Co.. p 85.

[109] Fleming, S. (187). *Uniform non-local time (terrestrial time)*, Ottawa, Canada,

1847, when Charles Dodgson was 15 years old, the railroad companies acted unilaterally to solve this problem by officially adopting Greenwich Mean Time, based on the location of the midday sun at the Royal Observatory in Greenwich, as the standard time across Great Britain. It would be more than 30 years before the country as a whole would follow suit, and, as you can imagine, people talked a lot about the pros and cons of the proposed changes before they came to pass.

By the time Dodgson was 17 years old, he had formulated the following "difficulties" regarding time, and had written them into his Rectory Umbrella, one of a series of family "magazines" which he produced to entertain his family at the Rectory.

Difficulties, No. 1 : Half of the world, or nearly so, is always in the light of the sun: as the world turns round, this hemisphere of light shifts round too, and passes over each part of it in succession.

Supposing on Tuesday, it is morning at London, in another hour it would be Tuesday morning at the west of England. If the whole world were land, we might go on tracing* Tuesday morning, Tuesday morning all the way round, till in twenty-four hours we get to London again. But we *know* that at London, 24 hours after Tuesday morning, it is Wednesday morning. Where then, in its passage round the earth, does the day change its name? Where does it lose its identity?

Practically there is no difficulty in it, because a great part of its journey is over water, and what it does out at sea no one can tell; and besides, there are so many different languages that it would be hopeless to attempt to trace the name of any one day all round. But is the case inconceivable that the same land and the same language should continue all round the

p 32

world? I cannot see that it is; in that case either there would be no distinction at all between each successive day, and so week, month &c. so that we should have to say 'the Battle of Waterloo happened to-day, about two million hours ago,' or some line would have to be fixed, where the change should take place, so that the inhabitants of one house would wake and say 'Heigh-ho!** Tuesday morning! And the inhabitants of the next, (over the line,) a few miles to the west would wake a few minutes afterwards and say 'Heigh-ho! Wednesday morning!' What hopeless confusion the people who happened to live on the line would always be in, it is not for me to say. There would be a quarrel every morning as to what the name of the day was to be. I can imagine no third case, unless everybody was allowed to choose for themselves, which state of things would be rather worse than either of the other two.

I am aware that this idea has been started before, namely, by the unknown author of that beautiful poem beginning, 'If all the world were apple pie,*** etc. The particular result here discussed does not appear to have occurred to him; as he confines himself to the difficulties in obtaining drink would certainly ensue.

Any good solution of the above difficulty will be thankfully received and inserted. The second 'difficulty' is one which would only appear to be difficult to a very young child, one would think, as it is purely a verbal complexity.

The *footnote adds: The best way is to imagine yourself walking round with the sun, and asking the inhabitants as you go, "What morning is this?" If you suppose them living all the way round, and all speaking one language, the difficulty is obvious.
The ** footnote adds: This is clearly an impossible case, and is only put as an hypothesis.

The *** footnote adds: If all the world were apple pie / And all the sea were ink / And all the trees were bread and cheese / What *should* we have to drink?

Difficulties, No. 2 : Which is the best: a clock that is right only once a year, or a clock that is right twice every day? "The latter," you reply, "unquestionably." Very good, reader, now attend.

I have two clocks: one doesn't go at all, and the other loses a minute a day" which would you prefer? "The losing one," you answer, "without a doubt." Now observe: the one which loses a minute a day has to lose twelve hours, or seven hundred and twenty minutes before it is right again, consequently it is only right once in two years, whereas the other is evidently right as often as the time it points to comes round, which happens twice a day. So you've contradicted yourself *once*: 'Ah, but' you say, 'What's the use of it being right twice a day, if I can't tell when the time comes?' Why, suppose the clock points to eight o'clock, don't you see that the clock is right *at* eight o'clock? Consequently when eight o'clock comes your clock is right. 'Yes, I see *that*,' you reply*. Very good, then you've contradicted yourself *twice*; now get out of the difficulty as you can, and don't contradict yourself if you can help it.

The * footnote adds: You *might* go on to ask, 'How am I to know when eight o'clock *does* come? My clock will not tell me.' Be patient, reader: you know that when eight o'clock comes your clock is right: very good; then your rule is this, keep your eye fixed on the clock, and *the very moment it is right* it will be eight o'clock. "But—"you say. There, that'll do, reader; the more you argue the farther you get from the point, so it will be as well to stop.

If you haven't noticed, the footnote to Difficulty No. 2 playfully likens the reader to a slow clock which would more likely be right if stopped, but despite this quip, there *are* specific "answers" to each difficulty, and we know this because the teenaged Charles Dodgson was not the originator of the difficulties, but more of an interpreter. Both difficulties are simplified, comedic versions of specific paradoxes presented by the mathematician and logician Augustus De Morgan.

The first difficulty, dealing with the start of the day on a revolving globe, complicated by a hypothetical traveler moving at the same speed as the sun overhead, *was* presented by De Morgan in his 1845 book, *The Globes, Celestial and Terrestrial.* The "answer" presented by De Morgan was that the "real solar day begins when the sun's centre is on the meridian" and that the traveler, "if he could move fast enough, he might keep the sun on his meridian, or, more properly, change meridians as fast as the sun, and have it always noon. . . . when he moves westward, he comes among those . . . whose watches are slower than his own, and the sun will set and rise by their watches, not by his; the contrary if he travels eastward."[110] This is a problem with which we are quite familiar and which we can easily understand due to our experiences with long distance air travel, but it was quite a novel question at the time.

The second difficulty, regarding the slow versus stopped clocks, was presented by De Morgan in his 1847 book, *Formal Logic: or, the Calculus of Inference, Necessary and Probable,* as an illustration of a logical fallacy based on the quantity of the proposition—"of things of the same kind, that which is sometimes right must be better than that which is always wrong." Those

---

[110] De Morgan, A. (1845). *The globes, celestial and terrestrial.* London: Malby and co., pp 71-73

unfamiliar with logical thinking might agree, "but," De Morgan stated, "a little consideration will suggest that what is always wrong may be as good as that which is sometimes right, if we do not know how to distinguish the cases in which the later is right; and also that what is not much wrong, generally, may be more usefull than that which is mostly very wrong, when it is not absolutely right. A watch which does not go is right twice a day; but it is not so useful as one which do go, though very badly."[111]

Dodgson continued to delight in posing his riddle, where does the day begin, for years, writing an open letter on the subject which was published on April 18, 1857, and which he signed, Mathematical Tutor, Oxford. A back and forth discussion began on the subject in *Notes and Queries*, a weekly publication of the Oxford University Press intended as "a medium of inter-communication" in which academics would pose open questions hoping for enlightening replies. Those writing in on the subject proposed fairly straightforward answers, such as that the beginning and ending of each day begins at every meridian successively, or that the day began at the meridian opposite to Greenwich at noon, but there was one man who wasn't satisfied with these rather straightforward answers. He responded, "Where does the Day being?—Every meridian on the globe has a certain moment on which any given day, say Sunday, November 29, begins. What meridian is the one on which that day begins at the earliest moment of absolute time?"[112] He signed himself only, "M."[113]

---

[111] De Morgan, A. (1847). *Formal logic: or, The Calculus of inference, necessary and probable*. London: Taylor and Walton, p 274

[112] p 498 Notes and queries, Second Series—Volume Sixth, July-December, 1858 London: Bell & Daldy. VI 155., Dec 18 '58 (1858)

[113] M also submitted a note less than a month earlier regarding the various ways very short periods of time are denoted, and adds, humorously "I am satisfied, from observation, that "less than no time" is much longer than "no

It is difficult to understand what M. (possibly Lewis Carroll himself) was getting at without a discussion of the different ways of measuring time, and the fact that what we commonly think of as a day, 24 hours commencing at midnight and based on the rising and setting of the sun, is really only an arbitrary measurement devised to average out days which are of unequal length because of the earths' elliptical orbit, and its difference in velocity at those times when it is nearer or farther from the sun. Because of these variations, real or apparent time (time based on our observation of the sun as it passes over the meridian of a place), and mean (averaged) time are only equal to each other 4 times in a year, on April 15th, June 15th, Sept 1st and Dec 24th. But even so, mean solar time does not precisely agree with the seasonal year, which is why we add a day to the calendar every 4th year to adjust to the correct time. Solar time is not as accurate as Sidereal time, which is time measured with reference to the apparent motion of a star passing a specific point in the sky. Time measured in this fashion will be accurate for thousands of years. But—it is difficult to correlate mean solar time and sidereal time, as the sidereal day is nearly 4 minutes shorter than the solar day, and this difference means that sidereal time tracks time independently of our day and night. In fact, mean solar time and sidereal time agree on only one day of the year, in March. Our clocks are, quite literally, "right only once a year." The calculation of when the day begins with regard to *absolute* time, sometimes called *mathematical* time[114], would have been so complex that it is easy to see how it could throw a damper on a dinner party.

---

time:" and I suspect that a brace of shakes must be the least time possible, because I have never heard of its being halved." 2nd Series, Vol. VI 152, Nov. 27 '58. P 437

[114] "Absolute, true and mathematical time, of itself, and from its own nature flows equally without regard to any thing external; and by another name is called Duration. Relative, apparent, and vulgar time, is some sensible and

As if that isn't complicated enough, just as the solar day varies from the sidereal or astronomical day, the moon has its own time, completing one sidereal revolution (a revolution from any given point to the same point again) in 27 1/3 days. In that vein, Alexander Taylor, the author of *The White Knight*, calculated the difference between the lunar and calendar months for the day of May 4, 1862, the day he believed the mad tea party was meant to have taken place, and found a two day difference, thereby accounting for the fact that the hatter's watch was two days late.[115] The late, great mathematician and science writer Martin Gardener, considering Taylor's claim, stated that "it is hard to believe Carroll had all this in mind."[116] But it would *not* have been the first time that a writer used the device of a man's watch running on lunar time and therefore running late compared to one running on solar time. That honor belongs to 1843's *The Commissioner; or De Lunatico Inquirendo*, and the Chevalier de Lunatico, with his black tights, and coat with buttons not unlike the star-studded sky of a clear night, his shirt with a frill like the edge of a white cloud, his "moonshiny" face, and his lunar time watch.[117]

I have introduced you to Dodgson's "difficulties" to prove that his infatuation with time more than rivaled that of Theophilus Carter, the anonymous Oxford furniture maker put forward as the hatter long after Lewis Carroll's death by H.W. Greene, a little

---

external measure of duration by motion, whether accurate or unequable, which is commonly used instead of true time; as an hour, a day, a month, a year." Newton, I. (1802). *Mathematical principles of natural philosophy.* The 2d ed. London: Printed by A. Strahan for T. Cadell & W. Davies. P 12.

[115] Taylor, A. L. (1952). *The white knight.* Edinburgh: Oliver & Boyd.

[116] Martin Gardner in The Annotated Alice (1960) New York: Bramhall House, p 96.

[117] James, G. P. R. 1801?-1860. (1843). *The commissioner: or, De lunatico inquirendo.* Dublin: W. Curry, pp 170-171.

known Oxford Classics professor, and the author of such forgettable poetry on the Oxford scene as, *A Welcome*, *The Way of the Wind*, and *Smiles that fade in tears*" ("So through the golden weather youth rejoices; But those whose spring is past Sit vainly listening for remembered voices Grown still at last.")[118] Eliminating Carter as a model for the Hatter brings us closer to our ultimate goal of determining who and what Lewis Carroll's Hatter was meant to represent, and what, *if anything*, the Hatter has to do with Mad Hatter's Disease, a phrase, the definition of which, is mercury poisoning?

---

[118] (1896). *More echoes from the Oxford magazine: being a second series of reprints of seven years.* London: H. Frowde, pp 49-49, 138, 142-143.

Mad as a Hatter

She's after that butterfly, mad as a hatter. [*It's not clear to me Why a hatter should be Proverbially called a fit subject for DeLunatico—so runs the writ—inquirendo; But I fancy the hatter this harsh innuendo Must, in the first place, to a humorous friend owe, Who fain in the sneer would his gratitude smother For a man who's invariably felt for another.*

-Tom Hood

Just as the phrase "mad as a March hare" had been around before Lewis Carroll was born, the phrase "mad as a hatter" had been around for many years before Lewis Carroll used it, or more specifically, did not use it. For, although the Cheshire cat informs Alice that both the March Hare and the Hatter are mad, Lewis Carroll refers only to the Hatter, and never to the *Mad* Hatter. As we know now, hatters were "mad" in much the same way the March hares were. They were timid most of the time—so shy and anxious with strangers that they would tremble if they thought you were watching them—but they could erupt in unexpected flares of anger. Their madness was caused by breathing in the mercury vapours that were formed in the process of felt hat manufacture.

In past centuries, felted hats had been made mostly from sheep's wool, camel's and goat's hair, cotton and silk, the curly texture of which made them easy to felt, but the French had developed a process of curling the ends of the straight hair of beaver, rabbit and hare which made it possible to use them in felting, and which resulted in soft, silky hats which were very much in demand. The French called the process secretage, and kept its details secret for many years, but the process made its way to England in the seventeenth century, along with the waves of French Protestants who fled France in search of religious freedom after Louis XIV reaffirmed France as a Catholic country.

We know this because the subject was discussed in a session of the British parliament in 1765. (The Parliamentary record reads: "We accidentally gained this manufacture from France, by the arrival of the French refugees, who flocked over hither in shoals, after the repeal of the edict of Nantes, in the year, 1685, and were well received, protected, and encouraged, even by our then king James the second, notwithstanding his being a bigoted papist; for as he seems to have been a man of strong passions, his zeal for promoting the trade and manufactures of his country, was equal to his zeal for propagating his religion..."[119])

Secretage involved brushing fur pelts with a watered down mercury solution, repeated several times in succession until approximately two-thirds of the length of the hairs were moistened. The amount of the solution needed depended on the quality of the pelt. If the hair was softer, less mercury was needed to curl the ends, if rigid, a little more. To aid the impregnation, the skins were put into a stove-room, and exposed to heat in proportion to the amount of mercury solution which had been used. A wetter skin required more heat, as it was important to adjust the heat so that the pelts would dry quickly enough, otherwise the mercury solution would not produce its curling effect.[120] It was in the course of drying and heating the pelts that the hatters were most exposed to the mercury vapor,

---

[119] Kimber, Isaac, 1692-1755, and Edward Kimber. *The London Magazine, Or, Gentleman's Monthly Intelligencer.* London: Printed for R. Baldwin, January 1765, The History of the last session of parliament, pp 172-175.
[120] Thomson, John. A Treatise On Hat-making And Felting: Including a Full Exposition of the Singular Properties of Fur, Wool, And Hair. Philadelphia: H.C. Baird; [etc., etc.], 1868.

something which was quite harmful to their emotional and physical health.

By the year 1790, the French were openly demanding that an alternate felting process be found, one less harmful to the health of the hatters.[121] The article in which the objection was published was translated and reprinted in an English Manufacturing periodical in 1795,

> *The application of the solution of mercury in aqua fortis, as before described, to that hair which is intended to be made into hats, is a very unwholesome operation to the workmen who are employed in it, on account of the mercurial vapours, which they cannot help breathing; it would therefore be a very useful object of enquiry, to endeavor to ascertain what particular alteration the mercurial solution produces in the hair by its application; or to try to produce the same alteration, or any other, provided its effect were the same with respect to felting, by means of substance, the use of which would not be so unwholesome.*

The French, who were at that time on the brink of a dramatic revolution in workers' rights, continued to condemn the use of mercury in felting as detrimental to the health of workers, stating in 1812 that the conservation of men is far more important than the advancement of industry ("La conservation des hommes est bien autrement importante que l'avancement des'arts.")[122] It is not clear that the *British*, who were heavy users of mercury in *medicine*, realized how dangerous the use of mercury in *hatting* was. There is, in fact, evidence that they believed that the problem was not the mercury itself, but a byproduct of nitrate.[123]

---

[121] Annales De Chimie Ou Recueil De Mémoires Concernant La Chimie Et Les Arts Qui En Dépendent. A Paris et se trouve à Londres: chez Joseph de Boffe. (1790 vol 6) p 311

[122] Annales Des Arts Et Manufactures. Paris: Au Bureau des Annales, Tome XLVI, 1812

By the year 1829 the phrase "mad as a hatter" was in common usage[124], and it became a quite popularly used phrase in the 1850s, but the Gentlemen Scholars of the English upper classes *had no idea* what it actually meant.

A query as to the origin and meaning of the phase first appeared in the pages of *Notes and Queries* in 1860 after a book published on the origins of English Proverbs and Proverbial Phrases failed to include it.[125] The query did not elicit a reply until after yet another popular book was published which used the phrase. Showing a profound lack of understanding of the nature of mercury poisoning in the hatting industry, the first respondent to venture an answer stated "One is at a loss to understand why a hatter should be made the type of insanity rather than a tailor or a shoemaker." For a variety of economic reasons outside the scope of this book, life had become so hard for the working class poor in England that the

---

[123] In 1845 a British physician, discussing the death of 3 hatters who had died after sleeping in an apartment where they had been preparing the mercury solution on the stove, stated, "They had incautiously exposed themselves too much to the fumes, which are disengaged during the preparation of nitrate of mercury for the operation of felting, and which are well known to be nitric oxide gas converted into nitrous acid vapour by contact with the air."Robert, Sir, 1797-1882. *A Treatise On Poisons In Relation to Medical Jurisprudence, Physiology, And the Practice of Physic.* 1st American from the 4th Edinburgh ed. Philadelphia: E. Barrington & G.D. Haswell, 1845.

[124] January–June 1829 issue of *Blackwood's Edinburgh Magazine*, headed Noctes Ambrocianæ. No. XL1V (three fictional characters in conversation refer to a man as "raving", "dementit" and "mad as a hatter."); The Clockmaker, 1835, Thomas Chandler Haliburton "*And with that he turned right round, and sat down to his map and never said another word, lookin' as mad as a hatter the whole blessed time*" and "*Father he larfed out like any thing; I thought he would never stop - and sister Sall got right up and walked out of the room, as mad as a hatter.*"

[125] Notes and queries. Fourth Series.—Volume Third. Jan-June 1869, London:Published at the Office, 43 Wellington Street, Strand, W.C., ser 4 vol 3 June 26, '69. Notes and Queries, ser 4 v 3 Jan-June 1869) A query as to the meaning of the phrase first appeared June 1860, 2nd series, vol 4, p 462, a book published on English Proverbs and Proverbial phrases failed to include the common saying, p 614

more privileged classes could not understand why one particular trade should be singled out as having a more difficult time than the others. The man posing the query supposed instead that the explanation might be language-based, writing that the similarity in sound of the French word huitre, to the English word hatter, might be the origin as the French had a saying that a weak minded person reasoned like an oyster, or huitre.[126]

The Huitre to Hatter suggestion did not gain traction, but it can quite easily be seen how it might have served as a stepping stone to the theory proposed in 1869 that "mad as a hatter" was a "tortured and persistant corruption" of the German name for adder : natter, in a progress from natter to atter to hatter, in a reference to the anger or madness of the easily infuriated snake.[127] Lewis Carroll "loved *Notes and Queries*" and kept a complete set in his library[128], and there is little doubt that he followed the "mad as a hatter" debate as it was taking place. Considering that the adder-hatter corruption theory was proposed *after* the publication of Alice's Adventures in Wonderland, but *before* the publication of *Through the Looking Glass*, it is conceivable that this theory might have served as the basis for Carroll's corruption of the names for the March Hare and the Hatter characters as Haigha and Hatta in *Through the Looking Glass*.

In general the phrase "mad as a hatter" was understood to refer to a person who was completely mad, and showed his madness by his actions, but the origin was obscure and much

---

[126] Notes and queries. Third Series.—Volume Fifth. Jan-June 1864, London:Published at the Office, 32 Wellington Street, Strand, W.C., Jan 2, '64, p 24

[127] *Notes and queries*. Fourth Series.—Volume Third. Jan-June 1869, London:Published at the Office, 43 Wellington Street, Strand, W.C., Jan 16 '69 p 64.

[128] Elton, O. (1906). *Frederick York Powell: a life and a selection from his letters and occasional writings Vol 2*, Oxford: The Clarendon Press, p 362

guessed at. In 1871 a reader suggested that the phrase referred to cabbage tree hat makers in Australia[129], and another wrote in to say that he had heard the phrase used by lead miners in Derbyshire and gold miners in Australia to refer to a loner, or solitary man, who works "under his own hat" because he is a little mad.[130] In 1888 it was proposed that the saying originated with the candidature of a hatter from the borough of Southwark 60 years previously, as the man, a Mr. Harris, proved to be completely out of his mind.[131] The Southwark hatter explanation fit the time period in which the phrase arose, but it did not satisfy the common mind. An understanding of the emotional effects of mercury exposure in the hatting industry would have rendered it a plausible explanation, but that understanding was not yet commonly known. Academics were *still* questioning the origin of the phrase "mad as a hatter" in the year 1900, when a man wrote in to *Notes and Queries* in search of a better answer than the prevailing hatter as a corruption of adder answer, which he deemed "preposterous".[132]

Even though we now know *without question* that hatters were made mad by mercury poisoning, the mad as an adder explanation is still in active competition as the origin of the phrase

---

[129] *Notes and queries.* Fourth Series.—Volume Eighth. July-Dec 1871, London:Published at the Office, 43 Wellington Street, Strand, W.C., Nov. 11 '71, As Mad as a Hatter, p 395

[130] *Notes and queries.* Fourth Series.—Volume Eighth. July-Dec 1871, London:Published at the Office, 43 Wellington Street, Strand, W.C., Dec. 9 '71, As Mad as a Hatter, p 489

[131] *Notes and queries.* Seventh Series.—Volume Sixth. July-Dec 1888, London: Published at the Office, 22, Took's Court, Chancery Lane, E.C. By John C. Francis. Aug 11 '88, p 107

[132] *Notes and queries.* Ninth Series.—Volume VI. July-Dec 1900, London: Published at the Office, Bream's Buildings, Chancery Lane, E.C. By John C. Francis. Dec 8, 1900, p 448 "Mad as a Hatter."—In what did this phrase originate? (No satisfactory explanation has been given, the assertion that (h)atter is a corruption of adder seeming preposterous.

mad as a hatter. Those who support it contend *erroneously* that mercury poisoning could not have been the origin as mercury was not yet used in hatting when the phrase arose. They couldn't be more wrong, however. Mercury had been used in hatting in Britain since the late 1600s, long before the phrase arose.

There is no indication that Lewis Carroll understood the secrets of felt hat manufacture, and no indication that his hatter character was meant to be suffering from mercury poisoning. There *is* plenty of evidence that the Hatter was introduced to answer the question, quite literally, for children in a way that would amuse them, of what would happen if you actually had control over time, of what could happen if you were on friendly terms with time, as opposed to what would happen if you could actually beat and murder it. But why a hatter?

The Fabric of Time

For what is Time? The shadow on the dial, — the striking of the clock, — the running of the sand, — day and night, — summer and winter, — months, years, centuries! These are but arbitrary and outward signs, — the measure of Time, not Time itself!

-Henry Wadsworth Longfellow

Thomas Carlyle was born the son of a stone mason turned farmer in 1795 in the South of Scotland. By the time he entered University, he was already the victim of a dyspeptic neurasthenia which was believed to have originated in his stomach and liver. As a result, he was hypersensitive to stimuli, unable to sleep or to bear excessive noise, "prey to nameless struggles and miseries" with "a kind of horror" in his thoughts.[133] As he prepared to seek medical care, he wrote beforehand to his father that he suspected that the doctor would advise him to "throw mercury into the system", and that is indeed what happened.[134] Carlyle would, in fact, continue to use mercury to address his biliousness and dyspepsia throughout his entire life.[135] Later Carlyle would write that, "Except for dyspepsia I could have been extremely content, but that did dismally forbid me now and

---

[133] *The Infirmities of Genius*, by W.R. Bett, (philosophical society, new York?) Christopher Johnson, London, 1952, Thomas Carlyle, A Victim of Dyspeptic Neurasthenia, pp11-22

[134] Carlyle, T. (1886). *Early letters of Thomas Carlyle.* London: Macmillan and co.. vol 2, pp 246-251

[135] There is overwhelming evidence that both Thomas Carlyle and his wife were habitual users of mercurial medications. Letters and Memorials of Jane Welsh Carlyle, New York, Charles Scribner's Sons, 1887, pp 80, 98, 137, 176, 211, 301, 357

afterwards! Irving and other friends always treated the 'ill-health' item as a light matter which would soon vanish from the account' but I had a presentiment that it would stay there, and be the Old Man of the Sea to me through life, as it has too tragically done, and will do to the end. Woe on it, and not for my own poor sake alone; and yet perhaps a benefit has been in it, priceless though hideously painful!"[136]

Carlyle believed that the abnormal sensitivity which he attributed to dyspepsia had contributed to his art, that his brilliant works had been stimulated by the irritant, the way an oyster forms a pearl. Gustave Flaubert, another brilliant writer who suffered from a variety of nervous disorders *disliked* the common understanding that sensitive nerves could "make a poet".

This confusion is a sacrilege," he wrote. "I can say something on the subject, I, who have heard people speaking in a low voice thirty yards off me through closed doors; I, whose viscera have been seen through my skin, leaping and bounding, who have at times felt in the space of a second thousands of thoughts, images, combinations of all kinds, which threw into my brain all at once, as it were, all the lighted squibs of a set piece of fireworks; but these are excellent moving subjects of conversation. Poetry is not a debility of the mind, and these nervous susceptibilities are. This faculty of abnormal perception is a weakness. I explain myself.

If I had had a sounder brain, I should not have made myself ill over reading law, and wearying myself; I should have made some profit out of it, instead of getting harm. The vexation instead of staying in my head passed into my limbs and made them writhe in convulsions. It was a deviation. There often appear children, who are made ill by music; they have great capacity for it, retain airs on the first hearing, become excited over playing the piano, their hearts beat, they become thin,

---

[136] *Reminiscences*, by Thomas Carlyle, Edited by james Anthony Froude, Vol I, London, Longmans, Green, and Co. 1881, P 200

pale, fall sick, and their poor nerves, like those of dogs, writhe in suffering at the sound of the notes. These are not the future Mozarts; the vocation has been misplaced; the idea has passed into the flesh, where it remains barren, and the flesh wastes; neither genius nor health are the outcome."[137]

Here, Flaubert is saying that his writing talent was *not* due to his abnormally sensitive temperament and that in most cases, the kind of nervous disorders that he was susceptible to did not lead to genius, but to ruin and waste. Still, it is hard not to read his comments about the thousands of thoughts firing in his brain all at once, and to suspect that it might, in his case, have contributed to his work.

In our day it is popularly understood that there is some connection between genius and madness, by which we generally mean the tendency to substance abuse and *mental* conditions including social deficits, depression, wild mood swings and delusions. In the 1800s they believed that madness was the end result on a continuum of *neurological* problems that plagued men of high ability in proportion greater than in the population as a whole, from those neurological problems likely arising from a degeneration occurring at a young age or before birth, such as physical asymmetry and stammer, to neurological perversions of appetite, right through to the tendency to paralytic afflictions.[138] In this, the geniuses had much in common with the insane, who were so commonly afflicted with paralysis that it was considered a natural conclusion of certain forms of nervous insanity and was termed, "the general paralysis of the insane." General Paralysis of

---

[137] Tarver, J. Charles. (1895). *Gustave Flaubert as seen in his works and correspondence.* New York: D. Appleton, pp 142-143
[138] The Man of Genius, by Cesare Lombroso, London, Walter Scott, 1891, Chapter II., Genius and Degeneration

the Insane was a steadily progressive disease which began with subtle disturbances of mental, sensory, or motor control. Tremor, clipping of words, and slight changes in gait were the most common initial physical symptoms, which might be accompanied by change in feeling, loss of sensation, and slight perversions in sight, such as color blindness.[139]   The accompanying mental disturbances included restlessness, depression, emotional instability, and loss of memory. As the disease progressed, there would be convulsive fits, and increasing blindness, deafness and loss of appetite.[140]   That these symptoms precisely describe the symptoms manifested by those overexposed to the neurotoxin mercury should come as no surprise, as the incredible amount of mercury used in medicine would have resulted in many such cases.

As for Carlyle, he wrote that "My own situation was very wretched; primarily from a state of health which nobody could be expected to understand or sympathise with, and about which I had as much as possible to be silent. The accursed hag 'Dyspepsia' had got me bitted and bridled, and was ever striving to make my waking living day a thing of ghastly nightmares."[141] But, at some point in his agitation and despair, Carlyle began to see the world differently. He took the bit in his mouth and broke free, his imagination no longer constrained by ordinary boundaries. In 1831 the 36 year old Carlyle published his book, *Sartor Resartus*

---

[139] Tests to determine impairment of color vision have been suggested as a reliable indicator of toxic levels of inorganic mercury in the system. Reversible color vision loss in occupational exposure to metallic mercury, Cavalleri A., Gobba F. Environ Res. 1998 May;77(2):173-7.

[140] Savage, G. Henry. (1884). *Insanity and allied neuroses: practical and clinical.* Philadelphia: Henry C. Lea's Son & Co.., Ch. XII General Paralysis of the Insane, pp. 276-350.

[141] Reminiscences, by Thomas Carlyle, Edited by james Anthony Froude, Vol I, London, Longmans, Green, and Co. 1881, P 241

(Tailor Retailored), in which a tailor by the name of Herr Teufelsdröckh grapples with issues of time and space, thereby forming a complicated philosophy of clothes.[142] It was Carlyle's philosophy, really. "I remember well enough," Carlyle wrote, "the very spot (at Templand) where the notion of astonishment at *clothes* first struck me."[143] Clothes, it struck him, were sewn from things taken from the earth, from things which once had been alive, and yet they were, as we are also, moving constantly to a state of disrepair. It was an idea which set Carlyle thinking about the way in which we and everything around us comes and goes— that permanence is an illusion which we harbor because we are here too briefly to see palaces and mountains coming and going.

Carlyle's philosophy of clothes was a thinly veiled metaphor for Kant's metaphysical philosophies that time and space are only constructs of our thoughts, or, as Carlyle put it in *Sartor Resartus*, that time and space are thought *woven*, so that our souls are *clothed* by time and space, a creation which, although it is beautiful, is a "dreamland" that limits us and blinds us to our true reality. Unaware of our true nature, our souls try to accommodate themselves to the conditions of this dreamland.

That we dream our lives and our world was said most beautifully by William Shakespeare in *The Tempest*, through Prospero , who exclaimed, "—These our actors, as I foretold you, were all Spirits, and are melted into Air, into thin Air; and like the baseless Fabric of Their Vision, the cloud-capt Towers, the gorgeous Palaces, the solemn Temples, the great Globe itself, yea all which it inherit, shall dissolve—and like this unsubstantial Pageant faded, leave not a rack behind! We are such stuff as

---

[142] Sartor Resartus: The Life and Opinions of Herr Teufelsdröckh, by Thomas Carlyle, London, Chapman and Hall, 1831

[143] Reminiscences, by Thomas Carlyle, Edited by james Anthony Froude, Vol I, London, Longmans, Green, and Co. 1881, P 302

dreams are made on, and our little life is rounded with a sleep." Carlyle both acknowledges Shakespeare and borrows from him, paraphrasing Shakespeare's Prospero to write, "We are such stuff as dreams are made of, and our little life is rounded with a sleep." Carlyle goes farther, however, to ask, if you could only tear apart the cloth of time and space and look through the weave, what would you find?

His answer was that if you looked beneath what we consider to be *real*, you would find madness, sometimes attributed to demons or spirits, and sometimes attributed to diseases of the nerves—a whole world of internal madness in every wisest Soul, and a chaos of madness below the habitable flowery rind of Earth.[144]

Considering that Carlyle's entire novel was based upon a metaphysical philosophy of clothes, it is not surprising that he would have included a bit on hats as a clothing based symbol of the power of our thoughts over time and space. There was already a precedent in a popular fantasy story called Old Fortunatus, about a man who had a purse providing limitless wealth, and a hat which could transport him anywhere he wished. "Fortunatus had a wishing Hat," Carlyle wrote, "which when he put on, and wished himself Anywhere, behold he was There. By this means had Fortunatus triumphed over Space, he had annihilated Space; for him there was no Where, but all was Here." It was easy enough for Carlyle to extend the allegory.

Were a Hatter to establish himself, in the Wahngasse of Weissnichtwo[145], and make felts of this sort for all mankind, what a world we should have of it! Still stranger, should, on the opposite side of the street, another Hatter establish himself; and, as his fellow-craftsman made Space-annihilitating Hats,

---

[144] Carlyle, T. (1831). *Sartor resartus: the life and opinions of Herr Teufelsdrœckh. In three books.* London: Chapman and Hall, p 207
[145] Delusion Alley of Know-not-where

make Time-annihilating! Of both would I purchase, were it with my last groschen; but chiefly of this latter. To clap-on your felt, and, simply by wishing that you were Anywhere, straightaway to be There! Next to clap-on your other felt, and, simply by wishing that you were Anywhen, straightaway to be Then![146]

In many respects, Thomas Carlyle's time-annihilating madness-revealing hatter was the first mad hatter in literature. It is always possible, of course, that Lewis Carroll designed his hatter character without reference to Thomas Carlyle's hatter, based solely on the vague but popular understanding that hatters were mad. How do we know that Lewis Carroll was even aware of Thomas Carlyle's Sartor Resartus? *Every* upperclass English school boy of Carroll's generation read, or tried to read Sartor Resartus.

That our own language contained a literature worthy of the deepest study was an idea which had not occurred at that time to any educationalist, however advanced; but, in some mysterious way, we picked up a sort of bowing acquaintance with Shakespeare and Tennyson and Pope and Byron, and read "Alton locke," and "Sartor Resartus".[147]

References to Carlyle's time-annihilating hat would pop up here and there in literature for quite some time before it was forgotten (1905: "the time-annihilating hat for which Carlyle sighs so vainly."[148] 1911: "But The Philosopher and I laugh up at [the stars], and plan how we will explore them all when we are free

[146] Sartor Resartus: The Life and Opinions of Herr Teufelsdrockh, by Thomas Carlyle, London, Chapman and Hall, 1831, Book III, Chapter VIII, Natural Supernaturalism, pp179-180
[147] The Amercian Catholic Quarterly Review, Vol XIII, 1888, Philadelphia, Hardy & Mahony, W. Marsham Adams "of a Past Generation"
[148] Anderton, I. Mary. (1905). *Tuscan folk-lore and sketches: together with some other papers.* London: A. Fairbairns

some day, making a grand tour among them—after we have donned the Time-annihilating Hat for which Teufelsdröckh longed, and have watched the solemn wonder of Creation and of Evolution upon this our own dear world."[149] 1912: "Could we by putting on Carlyle's Time-annihilating hat transport ourselves to ancient Greece, we should find the citizens believing themselves to be moderns."[150]) Carroll himself admitted to having read some (if not much) of Carlyle's *Sartor Resartus*, and to having thought over some of its basic ideas.

Letter to Edith Rix, Sept. 25, 1885 "My Dear Edith,--One subject you touch on—"the Resurrection of the Body"—is very interesting to me, and I have given it much thought (I mean long ago). My conclusion was to give up the literal meaning of the material body altogether. Identity, in some mysterious way, there evidently is; but there is no resisting the scientific fact that the actual material usable for physical bodies has been used over and over again—so that each atom would have several owners. . . I have read very little of "Sartor Resartus," and don't know the passage you quote: but I accept the idea of the material body being the "dress" of the spiritual—a dress needed for material life."[151]

In fact, Carlyle's terminology on the "annihilation" of time and space would often be used in the years long after *Sartor Resartus* was published, as various writers announced that it had been accomplished by the staggering new technologies coming into

[149] Sale, M. (1911). *A paradise in Portugal.* New York: The Baker & Taylor company, London: Andrew Melrose, p 30

[150] Harry Houdini Collection (Library of Congress), (1911). *The theosophical path.* Point Loma, Calif.: New Century Corp., Ancients, Moderns, and Posterity by Percy Leonard, p 21

[151] Collingwood, S. Dodgson. (1899). *The life and letters of Lewis Carroll (Rev. C.L. Dodgson).* New York: The Century Co., pp 241-242

existence, such as steam, electric wire and telegraph. In the years just before Lewis Carroll wrote *Alice's Adventures Underground*, an article in *The Leisure Hour*, describing these scientific advances, announced, "In a literal sense, it has realized the delirious demand of the poet; it has "annihilated time and space, and brought the distant regions of the continent, which were formerly months apart, and thousands of miles apart in space, into instant communion on one spot."[152] Another author wrote that "It has been said that railways and steam have annihilated space. It may be said that printing has annihilated time."[153]

Carlyle agreed with that last one. "In books lies the soul of the whole past time," he mused, "the articulate, audible voice of the past, when the body and material substance of it has altogether vanished like a dream."[154] Just like Lewis Carroll, who lives on in Alice's Adventures in Wonderland as the Mad Hatter, posing his riddles about time, ever so subtly, forevermore.

---

[152] *The Leisure hour: an illustrated magazine for home reading.* V. 5 (1856) London: [W. Stevens, printer, etc.], pp 723-733
[153] Lamartine, A. de. (1854). *Memoirs of celebrated characters 2d edition vol III.* London: R. Bentley, p 301
[154] Carlyle; Heroes and Hero Worship. The Hero as Man of Letters.

Nevar Written Backwards

"To the persevering mortal the blessed immortals are swift."
Yes, for they know how to give you in one moment the solution
of the riddle you have pondered for months.

-Ralph Waldo Emerson

In 1842, a 33 year old Edgar Allan Poe wrote a literary critique
of the 30 year old Charles Dickens' serialized novel, Barnaby
Rudge, pointing out many errors in plotting which lessened the
novel's suspense, and complaining that Dickens "had not
sufficiently considered or determined upon any particular plot
when he began the story."

"In tales of ordinary sequence he may and will long reign
triumphant. He has a talent for all things, but no positive genius
for adaption, and still less for the metaphysical art in which the
souls of all mysteries lie. "Caleb Williams" is a far less noble
work than "The Old Curiosity-Shop;" but Mr. Dickens could no
more have constructed the one than Mr. Godwin could have
dreamed of the other."[155]

Writing as you went along was common enough in the time
period, and it was especially common as writers contracted piece
work to be published on a weekly or monthly basis, and Dickens
was secure enough in his success not to be rattled by the
criticisms of a financially insecure and torqued up American poet.
Magnanimously, he sent Poe a friendly note in which he dropped

---

[155] *Graham's Lady's and Gentleman's Mmagazine.* (1842) vol 20-21
Philadelphia: George R. Graham & Co.,Review of New Books, Barnaby Rudge,
pp. 124- 129.

a line which would have tremendous impact on both Poe and Lewis Carroll's lives. "By the way," he wrote, "are you aware that Godwin wrote his 'Caleb Williams' backwards?"

It wasn't all in the sequence. It was obvious that if you knew where you were going, you could better build suspense, but this was something more, the idea that the art of writing could be approached in a calculated way, like a mathematical equation. With these thoughts in mind, Poe set out to craft a commercially successful poem. He decided first what length he should make his poem, by considering the "mathematical relation" of length in ratio to intensity, and aiming for a "degree of excitement" "not above the popular, while not below the critical taste." He concluded that his poem should be about 100 lines in length. ("It is in fact 108.") He next thought about the impression he wanted to convey, keeping always in mind his aim of creating a work which was *universally* appreciable." He chose Beauty as a subject with universal appeal, and sadness as the tone, and next decided to use a refrain because refrains were "so universally employed." Poe decided that his refrain would be the monotonously repeated word, "nevermore", and decided to use a Raven, a bird of ill omen, as a pretext for its continuous use.[156]

The Raven, published in 1845 was an immediate critical and commercial success. In 1846 Poe explained exactly how he had done it in an essay titled *The Philosophy of Composition*. Poe deconstructed "The Raven" to show how "the work proceeded, step by step, to its completion with the precision and rigid consequence of a mathematical problem." The secret, he explained, was that the end of every story must be conceived *first* so that every incident can contribute to the "development of the

---

[156] *Graham's American monthly magazine of literature, art, and fashion.* (1846) vol 28-29 Philadelphia: George R. Graham & Co., The Philosophy of Composition by Edgar A. Poe, pp 163-167

intention." He first established the climax. "Here then the poem may be said to have its beginning—at the end, where all works of art should begin—for it was here, at this point of my preconsiderations, that I first put pen to paper…"[157]

The Raven was so popular so quickly that parodies of it began to appear as early as the very year in which it was published, and the parodies kept coming, with countless variations of Poe's refrain, "nevermore" appearing in varied guise in refrains such as nevermore, never more, ever more, something more, nothing more, more and more, any-more, eat no more, pay your score, and never, sure!, written by scholars, wits, the institutionalized insane, and spiritualists who claimed to have contacted Poe's spirit from beyond the grave.[158]

The beyond the grave communications happened sooner, rather than later, for Poe did not live to appreciate his success for long. He died towards the end of 1849 under mysterious circumstances, found delirious and confused, and wearing a stranger's shabby clothes. He had been seriously ill rather recently with a suspected case of cholera for which he had been dosed half to death with calomel, as can be seen from this letter to a friend which Poe wrote on August 4, 1849, two months to the day before his death.

My Dear Sir,

The date of your last letter was June 7—so that two months have elapsed since you wrote it, and I am only just now sitting down to reply. The fault, Heaven knows, has not been mine. I

---

[157] Graham's American Monthly Magazine, Vol XXVIII (1846) Philadelphia: George R. Graham & Co., The Philosophy of Composition, by Edgar A. Poe, 163-167

[158] Hamilton, W. (1885). *Parodies of the works of English & American authors.* Vol 2, London: Reeves & Turner. p25–p103

have suffered worse than death—not so much from the Cholera as from its long-continued consequences in debility, and congestion of the brain—the latter, possibly, attributable to the calomel taken.

The last time Poe had been seen before he was found in en dishabille, he had been wearing a nice black suit and some said they had seen two rough looking men following him. In the interim, whatever happened, his clothes had been taken off of him and had been replaced by those of a man less well-off. He was found by a man who recognized him as the famous Poe, and who loaded him into a hackney carriage and directed the driver to bring him to the men's ward of Washington Medical College, a prison like ward for the care of the intemperate, whose windows were wired on the inside and grated on the outside.

The ward was overseen by a Dr. John J. Moran, who came forward, *thirty-five years* after Poe's death, with his recollections of those days in an attempt to salvage Poe's reputation. He had thought Poe might be drunk, he wrote, but on long reflection, he had come to realize that he had not been. For one thing, Poe had refused both the toddy and the opiates that were offered to him, he did not have tremor, and he did not smell of whiskey. [159]

In the late 1840's, the offer of opium and alcohol to those suffering from alcohol related delirium was customary practice, as standard treatment was a course of opium, ice to the head, beef-tea and stimulants. The delirium tremens, or D.T.s , were believed

---

[159] Moran, J. J. (1885). *A defense of Edgar Allan Poe: Life, character and dying declarations of the poet. An official account of his death.* Washington, D.C.: W.F. Boogher. Although Moran was resident physician of the hospital Poe was treated at, subsequent accounts have called into question the truth of some of the statements made in his account, especially Poe's deathbed statements, the florid details of which tend to raise suspicion that Moran's memories were embellished. Didier, E. Lemoine. (1909). *The Poe cult, and other Poe papers.* New York: Broadway publishing company.

to be a complex affectation of the nervous system characterized at first by an increased vascular excitement, and followed by a second stage in which the vital powers suffered a depression through the lack of alcohol, the accustomed stimulant. The first aim of treatment, therefore, was to lessen the excitement of the nervous system and to promote a restful sleep as the poison lessened in the body. This aim was traditionally served by the administration of opiates. The second stage, of therapeutic stimulants to restore nervous power, might be accomplished through gradually decreasing amounts of alcohol or by the use of mercurial stimulants, with some physicians recommending as much as 10 grains of calomel. [160] At any rate, it was generally considered to be of the utmost importance to keep the bowels open, which might also be accomplished with mercurials. We know from Dr. Moran's account that "Beef-tea and stimulants had been freely given and kept up at short intervals", but we don't know what those stimulants were. We do know that after 12 hours, Poe's color appeared to deepen, with "blood vessels at the temples slightly enlarging," an observation which implies that the stimulant Poe was given was believed to be capable of relieving congestion of blood and brain.

Poe had no idea what had happened to him. "My mind has kept no record of time," he was reputed to have said, "it seems a dream, a horrible dream." And it wasn't over yet, as a consulting physician, Dr. J. C. S. Monkur, a leading professor at the institution, confirmed Poe's fears that he was dying. It was Monkur's opinion that Poe was suffering from excessive nervous prostration, and loss of nerve power, and he advised the continuance of the remedies, including the beef tea and

---

[160] Tweedie, A. (1840) *Dissertations on Nervous Diseases Vol 2.* Philadelphia: Lea & Blanchard. Pp 225-248

stimulants. Very little remains of Dr. Monkur. He was Dr. John Cavendish Smith Monkur, a 48 year old Professor of medicine at the Washington University of Baltimore, known for his "bold and varied" therapeutics.[161] We know that he began his career at a drug and apothecary establishment, and that he was later a well-respected professor at Washington Medical, a college which failed and was disbanded a scant two years later, but we cannot recreate his usual practices, as he was "so constantly devoted to the practical duties of his vocation, that he had no time to contribute to the Literature of the Profession."[162] Can we draw any conclusions from the fact that Moran waited to publish his account until after Monkur was safely in the grave himself? Was he fairly laying blame on Monkur, or displacing his own blame? It was considered to be very difficult to distinguish delirium tremens from other conditions when there was no trembling, and a proper diagnosis required careful observation for several days. Moran's account emphasizes how careful his observation was, how necessary he felt it was to make a correct diagnosis, all very self-serving statements, but it should be emphasized, any guilt or blame that might be read between the lines of his account would have been that which he felt unfairly maligned the reputation of the great poet, and not that Poe had been given mercurial stimulants, if he had, as they would have been given under alternate diagnoses as well.

What happened to Poe? Rumors that mercury played a role in his ill-health in life have been quieted by reports that mercury found in his hair was not present in dangerous amounts, but

---

[161] Livingston, J. (1854). *Portraits of eminent Americans now living: with biographical and historical memoirs of their lives and actions.* New York: Cornish, Lamport & co.;London, S. Low, son & co.. John C. S. Monkur of Baltimore, Maryland, pp435-440

[162] *The Transactions of the American Medical Association Vol XVIII (1867).* Philadelphia: Printed for the Association by Collins. Pp 338-339.

those reports overlook the obvious, that the dramatic mercury exposure Poe experienced in the last months of his life would only have been present in new growth close to the scalp, and not in a sample taken from the ends of the hair (as Poe's was), and any exposure in the last few days of his life would not have appeared at all. It is a riddle, unanswerable, but not without an answer. We can only evaluate possibilities—of the answer itself we will be *never sure*.

Many people, hearing the Hatter's riddle, "Why is a raven like a writing desk?" have supposed it to have something to do with Edgar Allan Poe and his poem, *The Raven*, but haven't quite been able to work the riddle through. This is what we know: we know that Carroll wrote a story which parodied Poe's "nevermore" refrain years before he wrote his raven writing desk riddle (Carroll's 1856 *Novelty and Romancement* ends, "the signboard yet creaks upon the mouldering wall, but its sound shall make music in these ears nevermore—ah ! nevermore."), and we know that Carroll read Poe's *Philosophy of Composition* and that he took Poe's backward writing advice so dearly to heart that more than twenty years after *Alice*, he would ask one of his illustrators to illustrate in reverse sequence, to draw the last picture first and work backwards "as Poe tells us he wrote *The Raven*".

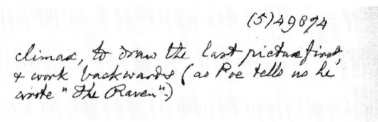

An excerpt of Carroll's letter to H. Furniss

The quest for a solution to the raven-writing desk riddle has been somewhat dampened by the in-text statements of both the

Hatter and the March Hare that they haven't the slightest idea what the answer is. Despite this, many men of proven ability have ventured a guess, including the American puzzle genius Sam Loyd (1841-1911), who wrote a variety of possible answers, such as "bills and tales are among their characteristics", "because they both stand on their legs", "because the notes for which they are noted are not noted for being musical notes", and "because Poe wrote on both."[163]

It is not difficult to overlook the Hatter's statement that he has no idea what the answer is—a joke or riddle is funnier if you get the answer yourself. An essay written in 1856 on the *Philosophy of Punning* (which Carroll, as an aspiring humor writer would almost certainly have read) made exactly that point, that puns presented and demanding a laugh are unlikely to get one. "They must be uttered in a peculiar way, so as to come on us with something of a surprise, and without any impertinent airs of consciousness."[164] Riddles were commonly posed in magazines of the day with the answers withheld pending a correct write-in solution by some savvy reader. Not only would allowing the reader to discover his own answer to the raven writing desk riddle heighten his appreciation of the riddle, having the Hatter pose a riddle without knowing the answer advances the story line. It would be a mistake, however, to assume that just because Lewis Carroll's *characters* didn't know the answer to the raven-writing desk riddle, that Carroll himself had no answer. *Does* Lewis Carroll's "why is a raven like a writing desk" riddle have an answer? Carroll was a mathematician, widely known to map out his life and his fiction in rigid complexities. He was more than

---

[163] Loyd, S. Cyclopedia of Puzzles (1914) p 114, as cited by Martin Gardner in The Annotated Alice (1960) New York: Bramhall House, p 95.

[164] *Putnam's Monthly Magazine..(1856) Vol VII.* New-York: Dix & Edwards, London: Sampson Low, Son & Co., The Philosophy of Punning, pp 154-166.

capable of running a text on more than one level, i.e., showing the hatter as the kind of man who asks riddles without answers to heighten the sense of lunacy, and of simultaneously crafting a clever riddle perfectly suited to the substance of his story. Nevertheless, the prevailing opinion today is that his Hatter riddle was never intended to have an answer, and those who believe it does *not* point not only to the Hatter's statement that he doesn't have "the slightest idea" of what the answer is, but also to a statement made by Carroll himself towards the end of his life, that "the Riddle, as originally invented, had no answer at all." That statement appeared in the preface of the 1896 Christmas edition of *Alice*, and read as follows,

> *Enquiries have been so often addressed to me, as to whether any answer to the Hatter's Riddle (see p. 97) can be imagined, that I may as well put on record here what seems to me to be a fairly appropriate answer, viz:* "Because it can produce a few notes, though they are <u>very</u> flat; and it is nevar *put with the wrong end in front!" This, however, is merely an* after-thought: the Riddle, as originally invented, had no answer at all.

Being somewhat contrary in nature, when I read this statement, all I can see is another clue. The wording is teasing. Nevar/raven backwards *feels* like a reference to Poe's Raven, those backwards and forwards mirror image words, as well as the bit about flat notes fits so perfectly into Carroll's puns about keeping and beating time in music and the greater issues of time in general that it does not seem as if it could be a solution contrived after the fact as Carroll appears to claim. There is a sense of something there, a sense of vague connection that leads people to keep guessing. Mark Richards of the UK Lewis Carroll society believes that this may be because Carroll had those connections in mind *subconsciously*. He writes,

> *If Carroll had no answer to the riddle when he posed it (as many of us believe), it still raises the question why did he choose the words "raven" and "writing-desk"? Even if consciously, he thought he was choosing two unconnected words – possibly just because of the alliteration, that does not mean they were not connected in his unconscious mind. He may well have had an image of Poe at a desk, writing the "Raven". And so, when looking for an answer to the riddle himself, it is natural to bring those subconscious thought to the front of the mind and come up with the "wrong end in front" answer.[165]*

The belief that the juxtaposition of images or ideas derived subconsciously can result in emotionally powerful connections is an axiom of surrealism, a movement which believes that as long as the connection is "true", the greater the distance between two "realities", "the stronger the image will be—the greater its emotional power and poetic reality."[166]   The implication of surrealism is that we are ordinarily so constrained by our conscious minds that where we would not ordinarily be able to make associations between distant images or ideas, that if we select objects in as thought-free a manner as we can achieve, we might subconsciously craft an unusual connection. Consider this quote from an early text attempting to define surrealism, "The surrealist object precedes definition, appears suddenly, alive and replete with suggestion for those who are predisposed to understand, as the solution of a complex problem suddenly reveals itself to those who have been concerned with that problem."[167] The fundamental premises of surrealism are solidly

---

[165] In a personal communication with the author, dated 3/26/14.
[166] Pierre Reverdy, Nord-Sud, March 1918.

in line with psychological theories which consider madness to be a failure of the *inhibition* of a constant boiling up of irrational thoughts. The surrealists are attempting to summon the spontaneous connections that genius makes beautifully and intentionally, and madmen, helplessly and erroneously.

Richards' suggestion is solidly in line with our understanding of Carroll's professions, made often *later* in his career that he used dream phrases which came to him without any understanding of their origin. But, like the surrealists, who would acknowledge Carroll as an early example of surrealism in nonsense, *earlier* in his career Carroll quite intentionally worked to bring these disparate images together.

While Carroll adopted Poe's *Philosophy of Composition* and attempted to follow its precepts throughout his life, there was another essay which he appears to have taken a decidedly antagonistic position against, an 1857 essay in *Fraser's Magazine* summarizing the earlier works of Archbishop Richard Whatley and Richard Chevenix Trench.[168] The article disparagingly addressed the trend among new writers of an affectation of a spasmodic style ("he will rather talk nonsense than not appear to be witty and original"), and implored would be writers *not* to attempt writing wit or humor unless they were born funny ("nascitur, non fit"), a reference to the common saying *poeta nascitur, non fit*, or the belief that a poet is *born*, and *not made*. Carroll, a new humor writer attempting a "spasmodic" style, appears to have taken the essay personally. As evidence, consider this excerpt of Carroll's early poem, *Poeta fit, non nascitur*[169], a title which translates to,

---

[167] Levy, J. (1936). *Surrealism.* New York: The Black sun press, pp 3-4.

[168] *Fraser's magazine.* Vol 55 (January to June, 1857) London: John W. Parker and Son, Literary Style pp

[169] *College Rhymes: Contributed by Members of the Universities of Oxford and Cambridge* Vol 3 (1862) Oxford: T. and G. Shrimpton. Cambridge: Macmillan and Co., pp. 112-116, author identified for unknown reasons as "K", but

the poet is *made*, and *not born*: in which an old man tells his grandson how to be a poet,

> *First learn to be spasmodic—*
> *A very simple rule.*
>
> *For first you write a sentence,*
> *And then you chop it small;*
> *Then mix the bits, and sort them out,*
> *Just as they chance to fall:*
> *The order that they come in*
> *Don't signify at all.*

One other reason Carroll may have taken so strongly against the essay is that it presumed to criticize a beloved comic writer, Thomas Hood, making derogatory references to the excessive publication of dull biographies and travel accounts, and making a not so veiled reference to the humourous travelogue "Up the Rhine" by Hood, the 1852 second edition of which contains the following note by the author in preface,

> *To be candid and confidential, the work was not offered to the public without some misgivings. A plain Manufacturer of Roman Cement, in the Greenwich road, was once turned by a cramped showboard into a "Manufacturer of Romancement;" and a Tour up the Rhine has generally been expected to convert an author into a dealer in the same commodity."*[170]

The joke Hood was making, like so many puns of the day, was dependent upon a loose similarity in words, so that roman cement, a form of mortar, was misunderstood to be

---

reprinted under Carroll's name in the later Rhyme and Reason, Carroll, L. (1884). *Rhyme? and reason?* New York: Macmillan and Co.., pp 123-130.

[170] Hood, T. (1852). *Up the Rhine.* Second edition. New York: G. P. Putnam and Son. p vi

"romancement" a non-existent word, but one which was suggestive of a material which might be used by novelists writing romances.[171] Confronted with the imagery of Hoods' roman cement and Trench's "tale of bricks", ("The Latin may contribute its tale of bricks, yes, of goodly and polished hewn stones, to the spiritual building; but the mortar, with all that hold and binds together the different parts of it together, and constitutes them into a house, is Saxon throughout."[172]), Carroll had begun to think in mathematical terms about what made nonsense, affectation and originality.

The leap Carroll made was that you might cement random ideas together, that chance ideas, *from whatever source*, might be cemented together like so many unrelated bricks into his own work, into his own "tale of bricks" (a term Carroll would use many years later to refer to his own work). The trick, of course, is how to do it, how to "link the unlinkable".[173] It is something which is not so easy to do well, and it is the subject of one of Carroll's earliest stories, the 1856, *Novelty and Romancement, A Broken Spell*[174]. I reproduce it here in full, as it provides a lot of insight into Carroll's early explorations of Noology, or the science of the mind, which holds that the primary function of the imagination is to conceive of analogies and relationships between objects external to the mind, and the ways in which this associative power can lead to false or absurd conclusions when unguided by logic and reason. As you read it, note the ways in which Carroll humorously portrays mans' tendency to misinterpret the world

---

[171] *The Knickerbocker; or, New-York monthly magazine..* Vol 22 (July – Dec 1843) New York: John Allen p 191

[172] *Fraser's magazine.* Vol 55 (January to June, 1857) London: John W. Parker and Son, p 436, Trench quoting an earlier passage on language made by Sir Thomas Browne

[173] Phrase quoted from Steve Martin's Born Standing Up.

[174] was published in *The Train*, volume 2, the July-Dec 1856 issue

around himself, from the narrator's unfounded dreams of grandeur, to the misreading of "signs" to find mystical meaning, to reading much, much more into a foreign language phrase book than was ever intended. Pay particular attention to Carroll's habit of frequent literary references and the way in which the story is set up for the conclusion it reaches. In many ways, the story can be seen as a precursor to *Alice*, for just as Alice wakes out of a dream she did not know she was having, the narrator in Novelty and Romancement wakes for a "dream" when he has to face certain truths.

Novelty and Romancement. A Broken Spell

by Lewis Carroll

I had grave doubts at first whether to call this passage of my life "A Wail," or "A Paean," so much does it contain that is great and glorious, so much that is somber and stern. Seeking for something which should be a sort of medium between the two. I decided, at last, on the above heading—wrongly, of course; I am always wrong: but let me be calm. It is a characteristic of the true orator never to yield to a burst of passion at the outset; the mildest of commonplaces are all he dare indulge in at first, and thence he mounts gradually;--*"vires acquirit eundo."* (See cover.) Suffice it, then, to say, in the first place, that *I am Leopold Edgar Stubbs.* I state this fact distinctly in commencing, to prevent all chance of the reader's confounding me either with the eminent shoemaker of that name, of Pottle-street, Camberwell, or with my less reputable, but more widely known, namesake, Stubbs, the light comedian, of the Provinces; both which connexions I repel with horror and disdain: no offence, however, being intended to either of the individuals named— men whom I have never seen, whom I hope I never shall.

So much for commonplaces.

Tell me now, oh ! man, wise in interpretation of dreams and omens, how it chanced that, on a Friday afternoon, turning suddenly out of Great Wattles-street, I should come into sudden and disagreeable collision with an humble individual of unprepossessing exterior, but with an eye that glowed with all the fire of genius? I had dreamed at night that the great idea of my life was to be fulfilled. What was the great idea of my life? I will tell you. With shame and sorrow I will tell you.

My thirst and passion from boyhood (predominating over the love of taws and running neck and neck with my appetite for toffee) has been for poetry—for poetry in its widest and wildest sense—for poetry untrammeled by the laws of sense, rhyme, or rhythm, soaring through the universe, and echoing the music of the spheres! From my youth, nay, from my very cradle, I have yearned for poetry, for beauty, for novelty, for romancement. When I say "yearned," I employ a word mildly expressive of what may be considered as an outline of my feelings in my calmer moments: it is about as capable of picturing the headlong impetuosity of my life-long enthusiasm as those unatomical paintings which adorn the outside of the Adelphi, representing Flexmore in one of the many conceivable attitudes into which the human frame has never yet been reduced, are of conveying to the speculative pit-goer a true idea of the feats performed by that extraordinary compound of humanity and Indian-rubber.

I have wandered from the point: that is a peculiarity, if I may be permitted to say so, incidental to life; and, as I remarked on an occasion which time will not suffer me more fully to specify, "what, after all, *is* life?" nor did I find any one of the individuals present (we were a party of nice, including the waiter, and it was while the soup was being removed that the above-recorded observation was made) capable of furnishing me with a rational answer to the question.

The verses which I wrote at an early period of life were eminently distinguished by a perfect freedom from conventionalism, and were thus unsuited to the present exactions of literature: in a future age they will be read and admired, "when Milton," as my venerable uncle has frequently exclaimed, "when Milton and such like is forgot!" Had it not been for this sympathetic relative, I firmly believe that the poetry of my nature would never have come out; I can still recall the feelings which thrilled me when he offered me sixpence for a rhyme to "despotism." I never succeeded, it is true, in finding the rhyme, but it was on the very next Wednesday that I penned my well known "Sonnet on a Dead Kitten," and in the course of a fortnight had commenced three epics, the titles of which I have unfortunately now forgotten.

Seven volumes of poetry have I given to an ungrateful world during my life; they have all shared the fate of true genius—obscurity and contempt. Not that any fault could be found with their contents; whatever their deficiencies may have been, *no reviewer has yet dared to criticize them.* This is a great fact.

The only composition of mine which has yet made any noise in the world, was a sonnet I addressed to one of the Corporation of Muggleton-cum-Swillside, on the occasion of his being selected Mayor of that town. It was largely circulated through private hands, and much talked of at the time; and through the subject of it, with characteristic vulgarity of mind, failed to appreciate the delicate compliments it involved, and indeed spoke of it rather disrespectfully than otherwise, I am inclined to think that it possesses all the elements of greatness. The concluding couplet was added at the suggestion of a friend, who assured me it was necessary to complete the sense, and in the point I deferred to his mature judgment:--

> "When Desolation snatched her tearful prey
> From the lorn empire of despairing day;
> When all the light, by gemless fancy thrown,
> Served but to animate the putrid stone;
> When monarchs, lessening on the wildered sight,
> Crumblingly vanished into utter night;
> When murder stalked with thirstier strides abroad,
> And redly flashed the never-sated sword;
> In such an hour thy greatness had been seen—
> That is, if such an hour had ever been—
> In such an hour thy praises will be sung,

> If not my mine, by many a worthier tongue;
> And thou will be gazed upon by wondering men,
> When such an hour arrives, but not till then!"

Alfred Tennyson is Poet Laureate, and it is not for me to dispute his claim to that eminent position; still I cannot help thinking, that if the Government had only come forward candidly at the time, and thrown the thing open to general competition (say "Frampton's Pill of Health, an Ancrostic"), a very different result might have been arrived at.

But let us return to our muttons (as our noble allies do most unromantically express themselves), and to the mechanic of Great Wattles-street. He was coming out of a small shop—rudely built it was, dilapidated exceedingly, and in its general appearance seedy—what did I see in all this to inspire a belief that a great epoch in my existence had arrived? Reader, I saw the sign board!

Yes. Upon the rusty signboard, creaking awkwardly on its one hinge against the mouldering wall, was an inscription which thrilled me from head to foot with unwonted excitement. "Simon Lubkin. Dealer in Romancement." Those were the very words.

It was Friday, the fourth of June, half-past four, p.m.

Three times I read that inscription through, and then took out my pocketbook, and copied it on the spot; the mechanic regarding me during the whole proceeding with a stare of serious and (as I thought at the time) respectful astonishment.

I stopped that mechanic, and entered into conversation with him: years of agony since then have gradually branded that scene upon my writhing heart, and I can repeat all that passed, word for word.

Did the mechanic (this was my first questions) possess a kindred soul, or did he not?

Mechanic didn't know as he did.

Was he aware (this with thrilling emphasis) of the meaning of that glorious inscription upon his sideboard?

Bless you, mechanic knew all about there 'ere.

Would mechanic (overlooking the suddenness of the invitation) object to adjourn to the neighboring public-house, and there discuss the point more at leisure?

Mechanic would *not* object to a drain. On the contrary.

(Adjournment accordingly: brandy-and-water for two: conversation resumed).

Did the article sell well, especially with the *"mobile vulgus?"*

Mechanic cast a look of good-natured pity on the questioner: the article sold well, he said, and the vulgars bought it most.

Why not add "Novelty" to the inscription? (This was a critical moment: I trembled as I asked the question.)

Not so bad an idea, mechanic thought: time was, it might have answered; but time flies, you see.

Was mechanic alone in his glory, or was there any one else who dealt as largely in the article?

Mechanic would pound it there was none.

What was the article employed for? (I brought this question out with a gasp, excitement almost choking my utterance.)

It would piece a'most anything together, mechanic believed, and make it soldier nor stone.

This was a sentence difficult of interpretation. I thought it over a little, and then said, doubtfully, "you mean, I presume, that it serves to connect the broken threads of human destiny ? to invest with a—with a sort of vital reality the chimerical products of a fertile imagination?"

Mechanic's answer was short and anything but encouraging: "mought be--. I's no scollard, bless you."

At this point conversation certainly began to flag; I was seriously debating in my own mind whether this could really be the fulfilment of my life-cherished dream; so ill did the scene harmonise with my ideas of romance, and so painfully did I feel my companion's lack of sympathy in the enthusiasm of my nature—an enthusiasm which has found vent, ere now, in actions which the thoughtless crowd have too often attributed to mere eccentricity.

I have risen with the lark—"day's sweet harbinger"—(once, certainly, if not oftener), with the aid of a patent alarum, and have gone forth at that unseemly hour, much to the astonishment of the housemaid cleaning the door steps, to "brush with hasty steps the dewy lawn," and have witnessed the golden dawn with eyes yet half-closed in sleep (I have always stated to my friends, in any allusion to the subject, that my raptures at that moment were such that I have never since ventured to expose myself to the influence of excitement so dangerous. In confidence, however, I admit that the reality did not come up to the idea I had formed of it over night, and by no means repaid the struggle of getting out of bed so early).

I have wandered in the solemn woods at night, and bent me o'er the moss-grown fountain, to lave in its crystal stream my tangled locks and fevered brow. (What though I was laid up with a severe cold in consequence, and that my hair was out of curl for a week? Do paltry considerations such as these, I ask, affect the poetry of the incident?)

I have thrown open my small, but neatly furnished, cottage tenement, in the neighbourhood of St. John's Wood, and invited an aged beggar in to "sit by my fire, and talk the night away." (It was immediately after reading Goldsmith's "Deserted Village." True it is that he told me nothing interesting, and that he took the hall-clock with him when he departed in the morning; still my uncle has always said that he wishes he had been there, and that it displayed in me a freshness and greenness of fancy (or "disposition," I forget which) such as he had never expected to see).

I feel that it is incumbent on me to enter more fully into this latter topic—the personal history of my uncle: the world will one day learn to revere the talents of that wonderful man, though a want of funds prevents, at present, the publication of the great system of philosophy of which he is the inventor. Meanwhile, out of the mass of priceless manuscripts which he has bequeathed to an ungrateful nation, I will venture one striking specimen. And when the day arrives that my poetry is appreciated by the world at large (distant though it now appear!) then, I feel assured, shall his genius also receive its meed of fame!

Among the papers of that respected relative, I find what appears to have been a leaf torn from some philosophical work of the day: the following passage is scored. "Is this your rose? It is mine. It is yours. Are these your houses? They are mine. Give to me (of) the bread. She have him a box on the ear." Against this occurs a marginal note in my uncles hand writing; "some call this unconnected writing: I have my own opinion." This last was a favourite expression of his, veiling a profundity of ethical acumen on which it would be vain to speculate; indeed, so uniformly simple was the language of this great man, that no one besides myself ever suspected his possessing more than the ordinary share of human intellect.

May I, however, venture to express what I believe would have been my uncle's interpretation of this remarkable passage? It appears that the writer intended to distinguish the provinces of Poetry, Real Property, and Personal Property. The inquirer touches first on flowers, and with what a gush of generous feeling does the answer break upon him! "It is mine. It is yours." That is the beautiful, the true, the good; these are not hampered by petty considerations of "meum" and "tuum;" these are the common property of man. (It was with some such idea as this that I drew up the once celebrated bill, entitled "An Act for exempting Pheasants from the operation of the Game Laws, on the ground of Beauty"—a bill which would, doubtless, have passed both Houses in triumph, but that the member who had undertaken the care of it was unfortunately incarcerated in a Lunatic Asylum before it had reached the second reading). Encouraged by the success of his first question, our inquirer passes on to "houses" ("Real Property," you will observe); he is here met by the stern, chilling answer, "They are mine"—none of the liberal sentiment which dictated the former reply, but in its place a dignified assertion of the rights of property.

Had this been a genuine Socratic dialogue, and not merely a modern imitation, the inquirer would have probably here interrupted with "To me indeed," or, "I, for my part," or "But how otherwise?" or some other of these singular expression, with which Plato makes his characters display at once their blind acquiescence in their instructor's opinions, and their utter inability to express themselves grammatically. But the writer takes another line of thought; the bold inquirer, undeterred by the coldness of the last reply, proceeds from questions to demands, "give me (of) the bread;" and here the conversation abruptly ceases, but the moral of the whole is pointed in the narrative; "she gave him a box on the ear." This is not the philosophy of one individual or nation, the sentiment is, if I may so say, European; and I am borne out in this theory by the fact that the book has evidently been printed in three parallel columns, English, French, and German.

Such a man was my uncle; and with such a man did I resolve to confront the suspected mechanic. I appointed the following morning for an interview, when I would personally inspect "the article" (I could not bring myself to utter the beloved word itself). I passed a restless and feverish night, crushed by a sense of the approaching crisis.

The hour came at last—the hour of misery and despair; it always does so, it cannot be put off for ever; even on a visit to a dentist, as my childhood can attest with bitter experience, we are not for ever getting there; the fatal door too surely dawns upon us, and our heart, which for the last half hour has been gradually sinking lower and lower, until we almost doubt its existence, vanishes suddenly downwards into depths hitherto undreamed of. As so, I repeat it, the hour came at last.

Standing before that base mechanic's door, with a throbbing and expectant heart, my eye chanced to fall once more upon that signboard, once more I perused its strange inscription. Oh ! fatal change! Oh ! horror! What do I see? Have I been deluded by a heated imagination? A hideous gap yawns between the N and the C, making it not one word but two!

And the dream was over.

At the corner of the street I turned to take a sad fond look at the spectre of a phantom hope, I once had held so dear. "Adieu!" I whispered; this was all the last farewell I took, and I leant upon my walking-stick and wiped away a tear. On the following day I entered into commercial relations with the firm of Dumpy and Spagg, wholesale dealers in the wine and spirit department.

The signboard yet creaks upon the mouldering wall, but its sound shall make music in these ears nevermore—ah ! nevermore.

For your amusement, and as an example of the sort of phrase book which the story's narrator read too much into, I have included a passage from an 1830 dictionary of French to English idioms which contains the phrase, "she gave him a box on the ear."[175]

COUVÈR—Il y a quelque chose qui couve.	*There is something brooding.*
Il couve quelque maladie.	*He is breeding some distemper.*
Ils couvent quelques mauvais desseins.	*They are hatching some mischief.*
COUVRIR—Elle lui couvrit la figure d'un soufflet.	*She gave him a box on the ear.*
CRACHÉ—Cet enfant est son père tout craché.	*This child is the very image of his father.*
CRACHER—Il crache en l'air, et cela lui retombera sur le nez.	*He digs a pit, and he will fall into it himself.*

If you read through it, you can see how, in an imaginative frame of mind, you could weave these unrelated, alphabetically

[175] Bellenger, W. A. (1830). *A dictionary of idioms: French and English.* 2d ed., corr. and very considerably enl.; London: Printed for Sherwood, Gilbert and Piper, p 60

arranged, idioms together into a story. Compellingly, this section of Carroll's story mirrors an incoherent book of disconnected sentences by an obviously insane man which had been making the rounds through the lunacy commissioners at the time, and which contained a long passage of grammar detailing phrases most of which were regarding the ownership of houses, such as "This house is mine; that (house) is yours. These or those houses are his. Whose are those?"[176] Knowing Carroll's habit of recording amusing or piquant conversation and including it in his fiction, it becomes too easy to imagine the conversation of narrator and uncle as the actual conversation of Carroll and his Uncle Skeffington laughing over the lunatic's book. Of course, the most interesting aspect of the story for our purposes is its ending, in which the narrator has to face that he has lost his dream of "romancement" in a repetitive use of the word "nevermore" which is so evocative of Poe's Raven.

Carroll was proud of the difficulty of his riddles. In 1897, in the last year of his life, he wrote, "Made a splendid logic problem, about "great-grandsons" (modelled on one by De Morgan). My method of solution is quite new, and I greatly doubt if any one will solve the Problem."[177] So it is that after he died, people began looking back on some of his unsolved riddles, expressing how sure they were that his reasoning must be fantastic, that there must be an answer, and that he would have always had an answer in mind.

---

[176] ("nearly thirty pages of disconnected and incoherent sentences, made more confusing still by the constant interpolation of synonyms, abbreviations without method, and other extravagences." p43 plain talk about insanity); *The age of words and phrases: A book for persons who undervalue themselves and overvalue others.* Boston: Printed by A. Mudge & son, intended, in the authors words, as "A work which is valuable to peculiar, sensitive, retiring, bashful, irresolute, hesitating, doubting, wavering minds."
[177] Collingwood, S. Dodgson. (1899). *The life and letters of Lewis Carroll (Rev. C.L. Dodgson).* New York: The Century Co.., p 336

One man, writing on pseudonyms in *The Science of Anonymity* wrote that "Lewis Carroll cannot be doubted to have manufactured that name by some fantastic reasoning out of his every-day Charles Lutwidge Dodgson."[178] The author did not yet know the details of the intricate way in which Lewis Carroll had, indeed, used fantastic reasoning to conjure his pen name out of "his every-day Charles Lutwidge Dodgson"—that would not become common knowledge until the following year when Carroll's nephew, Stuart Collingwood, would publish the first Lewis Carroll biography—but he knew Lewis Carroll well enough to be *sure* that it must be so. He was right, of course. As you may recall, Carroll had translated Charles Lutwidge into Carolus Ludovicus, and back again into Carroll Lewis, which he then inverted to produce Lewis Carroll. Some of Carroll's other pseudonyms, B.B., K., M. (possibly), R.W.G. (the fourth letters of each of his names), D. C. L., (both De Ciel, and Dodgson, Charles Lutwidge as his name would appear in a roster) and Mathematicus.

Similarly, after Carroll's death, his nephew wrote a short piece on his life for *The Strand Magazine*, concluding it with an extract from his juvenile production, "Misch-Masch", "a riddle", Collingwood wrote, "to which I for one do not know the answer. I can only hope, for the future sanity of any who may attempt to solve it, that it does not belong to the same class of conundrums as "Why is a raven like a writing-desk?"—

---

[178] *Good words.* Vol 39 (1898)edited by Donald MacLeod D.D., London: J. Strahan and Company Limited, The Science of Anonymity by Harry Smith, pp 99-104, p 104.

A monument—men all agree—
Am I in all sincerity;
Half cat, half hindrance made,
If head and tail removed should be,
Then most of all you strengthen me'
Replace my head, the stand you see
On which my tail is laid.[179]

Carroll's next biographer, Belle Moses, repeated the riddle with the plaintive statement, "there must be an answer, and it is therefore worthwhile guessing, for Lewis Carroll would never have written a riddle without one."[180] The thing about riddles is that the response to proposed answers is so individual. The punsters of the 1800s had reduced punning to a system, publishing dictionaries of possible puns by going through the dictionary A to Z and listing those words which sounded alike.[181] Slight differences in pronunciation were not only acceptable, but often the foundation of the trickier puns. Tables with words which sounded alike, but which had different meanings would list words as similar as cause and caws, ceiling and sealing, sear and seer, or as differing as salary and celery, correspondence and correspondents, descent and dissent, groan and grown, tray and trey, and, depending on dialect, as ant, aunt and haunt, edge and hedge, elm and helm, suitor and suture (Hatter and Hatta, Hare and Haigha), or those which were merely similar enough to get a laugh, like Employ and Imply, pear and pay'er, raisin and reason.[182]

[179] *The Strand Magazine.* (1898) vol 16 London: G. Newnes, LTD., Before "Alice"—The Boyhood of Lewis Carroll, pp 616-627.
[180] Moses, B. (1910). *Lewis Carroll in wonderland and at home: the story of his life.* New York: D. Appleton, p 63.
[181] Marryat, F. (1837). *The old commodore.* Paris: Baudry's European Library. Pp 305-306 (a fictional version, compiled and rented out.)
[182] Ashton, o. Liverpool. [from old catalog]. (1826). *The new expostior,* Rev., 39th ed. London: Printed for G. Cowie. A Table of Words Alike in Sound, pp

One of the "excruciating" riddles of the time was, Why is a lady wearing tight shoes like a vegetable?—Because she is a toe-martyr (tomato).[183]

With the ground prepared, and the foundation laid, so to speak, consider the following possible solution to Carroll's Misch-Masch riddle: *Ke'y* as a corruption of Kitty. Stonewall as a hinderance made. If Ke'y and wall removed should be, you have stone ("you strengthen me"), replacing the head, you have *keystone*, the structural support for a *wall*—the whole thing Ke'ystonewall, and the answer, a dialect corruption of Kedleston Hall. Kedleston Hall is a palatial English Country House in Kedleston, Derbyshire, which was the seat of the Curzon family. (A name very similar in sound to the Spanish word corazón, meaning heart, the source of sincerity.) Why a riddle on Kedleston Hall? Lewis Carroll attended Rugby as a boy with the Curzon boys from Kedleston Hall.[184] To those who believe this solution relies too much on dialect corruption, I would suggest, Carroll was only little more than a boy when he wrote it, and that his riddles were going to get better.

Discussing yet another unguessed riddle in the preface to *A Tangled Tale*, published in 1886, Carroll wrote, "Neither of them has guessed it: and this is true human nature. Only the other day—the 31st of September, to be quite exact—I met my old friend Brown, and gave him a riddle I had just heard. With one great effort of his colossal mind Brown guessed it. "Right!" said I.

118-132

[183] (1849). *The Schoolfello: A Magazine for Boys and Girls.* Vol. 6 (1854) New York: Evans and Dickerson, p 359

[184] Alfred Nathaniel Holden Curzon, of Kedleston Hall, attended Rugby age 12 in 1844. (p249) He would attend Merton College, Oxford, and become Rector of Kedleston in 1856. Dodgson entered aged 14, Jan 27 in 1846. Rugby School., . (1886). *Rugby school register, from 1675 to 1874 inclusive: with annotations and alphabetical index.* Rugby: A. J. Lawrence.

"Ah," said he, "it's very neat—very neat. And it isn't an answer that would occur to everybody. Very neat indeed." A few yards further on, I fell in with Smith and to him I propounded the same riddle. He frowned over it for a minute, and then gave it up. Meekly I faltered out the answer. "A poor thing, sir!" Smith growled, as he turned away. "A very poor thing! I wonder you care to repeat such rubbish!" Yet Smith's mind is, if possible, even more colossal than Browns."[185]

Of course, September has only 30 days.

Let's look at Carroll's disavowal/clue again,

"Because it can produce a few notes, though they are very flat; and it is nevar put with the wrong end in front!" This, however, is merely an after-thought: the Riddle, as originally invented, had no answer at all.

Very of <u>very</u> flat is underlined, most likely to encourage the reader to imagine flat notes made of paper in addition to the flat musical notes which would most likely be the first sort of flat notes to come to mind. Nevar is italicized to draw attention to the fact that it is not the word never, but *nevar*, or raven backwards. But why write the cumbersome "wrong end in front" instead of backwards?   Both Poe and Carroll used the word backwards when referring to the way Poe wrote *The Raven*. Why say "originally invented" instead of written? Might it have been that Carroll (needing an original riddle no one had ever heard before, and perhaps wanting to use raven nevar) began by testing a variety of why-is-a-raven-like riddles until he came up with why is a raven like a writing desk, and intuited an answer for it *before* he wrote it down? Lewis Carroll was adept at and proud of his

---

[185] Carroll, L. 1832-1898. (1886). *A tangled tale.* London: Macmillan., pp 125-126.

ability to misdirect through the use of literal truth. (According to the Hon. Lionel A. Tollemache, who knew Carroll from Oxford, wrote that Carroll would suggest that "if a dull writer sent you a copy of his books, you should at once write and thank him, and should add, with delphic ambiguity, that you will *lose* no time in perusing them!"[186]) Why capitalize Riddle? Was Riddle, capitalized, meant to refer to a fundamental riddle without an answer? [187] Consider a second excerpt from his *Poeta Fit, Non Nascitur*,

> *Then if you'd be impressive,*
> *Remember what I say,*
> *That abstract qualities begin*
> *With capitals alway:*
> *The True, the Good, the Beautiful,*
> *Those are the things that pay.*[188]

Did he say "wrong end in front" because to say "backwards" would give the riddle away too easily? And for that matter, Carroll's answer is in two parts, the first, about flat notes refers both to ravens and writing desks, but the second is missing the associated answer for writing desks. Why is that? There is no sense going farther, those who see the statement as a clue will be convinced that there is an answer to the riddle, and those see is as a disavowal will not be persuaded. At the very least, scholars should dial back their pronouncements that no answer was ever

---

[186] Tollemache, L. A. 1838-1919. (1908). *Old and odd memories.* London: Edward Arnold. P 311

[187] For example, when Lewis Carroll wrote this preface, a fellow Oxford Don had given a sermon a few years earlier in which he referred to the riddle of Job's suffering as having "no direct answer at all." Bradley, G. Granville. (1888) *Lectures on the Book of Job.* 2d ed. Oxford: Clarendon Press, p 326

[188] [188] *College Rhymes: Contributed by Members of the Universities of Oxford and Cambridge* Vol 3 (1862) Oxford: T. and G. Shrimpton. Cambridge: Macmillan and Co.,, Poeta Fit, Non Nascitur, p 113

intended and acknowledge that whether or not you believe there is an answer to the riddle depends entirely on the interpretation of this one statement.

When I first set out to solve Lewis Carroll's riddle, I believed that an answer could be made that would, if it fit precisely, be acknowledged as likely correct. I know now that is not possible. There is no answer that will ever be found sufficiently true. How can we say, yes, that is what he had in mind? In a very real way, that is a problem with this book as a whole, with my attempt to solve the riddle of Lewis Carroll's life. We can't know the truth of another's mind, or the truth of the past, but both have a truth nonetheless.

I persist in the belief that Lewis Carroll had an answer in mind when he *wrote* the raven-writing desk riddle, and that its genesis had something to do with Poe's poem *The Raven* (as so many have suspected), and his *Philosophy of Composition* (which Carroll took so closely to heart). It may be an answer as cerebral as "because Poe wrote on both backwards," which is very close to one of the solutions ventured by the American puzzle and chess genius Sam Loyd, but realistically, as Carroll was writing for children, it is probably something pun-tastic like, because a raven is nevar backwards, and a writing desk is always *for words*.[189]

---

[189] *Italicizing* a pun, the written equivalent of cuing that a pun has been made is "a gross offense, and punishable." *Putnam's Monthly Magazine..(1856) Vol VII.* New-York: Dix & Edwards, London: Sampson Low, Son & Co., The Philosophy of Punning, p 165.

Part III

Conclusions

Literally Mad

"Isn't it sad," she said, "about poor Mr. Lewis Carroll? He's gone mad, you know." "Indeed," replied Mr. Dodgson, "I had never heard that." "Oh, I assure you it is quite true," the lady answered. "I have it on the best authority."

-Woman on a Train
Unaware with Whom She was Speaking

In the year 2000, Lewis Carroll's Mad Hatter was discussed in a hearing on Mercury in Medicine held before the House of Representatives. The author of the report was trying to make the point that the overt symptoms of autism spectrum disorder and the symptoms of mercury poisoning are "strikingly similar," with both exhibiting psychiatric disturbances in a spectrum which includes social withdrawal, anxiety, irritability and depression, and physical disturbances such as hyper-arousal, difficulty sleeping, problems with articulation in speech, mild to profound hearing loss, incoordination or jerkiness in gait, and impaired face recognition, with the more severely affected exhibiting compulsive, schizoid and psychotic tendencies. Neuronal disorganization is seen in both, along with abnormalities in neurochemistry, including abnormal EEG's and epileptiform activity.[190] The report contains a very interesting comparison of the speech patterns and interests of an autistic adult named

---

[190] United States. Congress. House. Committee on Government Reform., . (2001). *Mercury in medicine--are we taking unnecessary risks?: hearing before the Committee on Government Reform, House of Representatives, One Hundred Sixth Congress, second session, July 18, 2000.* Washington: U.S. G.P.O. , table of abnormalities pp 33-36.

Lenny and the Mad Hatter, detailing especially, Lenny's rigid literal interpretation of word meanings, such as the following,

> *He was very literal minded, and words spoken to him became matters of immutable fact. For example, he was trying on new shoes. His mother asked him if they slipped up and down. He said they didn't, and when asked again if he were sure, he replied, 'No, they don't slip up and down; they slip down and then they slip up."*[191]

Lenny's literality was compared to that of the Hatter in the following conversation at the Mad Tea Party:

> *"Take some more tea," the March Hare said to Alice, very earnestly.*

> *"I've had nothing yet," Alice replied in an offended tone: "so I can'n't take more."*

> *"You mean you ca'n't take less," said the Hatter. "It's very easy to take more than nothing."*

It is a very interesting comparison, except that it presumes that the Mad Hatter suffered from occupational mercury exposure which we have seen is not likely so. But was the author of this report wrong in noticing similarities between the mercury exposed and the Hatter? Perhaps not, if the Hatter was Carroll and Carroll was overexposed to mercury himself. For all the ways that Carroll's *Hatter* talked, Carroll *himself* was known to talk.

> *"All he said, all his oddities and clever things, arose out of the conversation—conversation quite of an ordinary everyday sort; to explain it at all you would want shorthand notes of everything that was said, and even then you would not follow it, unless you*

---

[191] Ibid, p 44.

knew the people who were talking, the peculiarities of this man, and the deafness of that, and so on. It was Alice, all kinds of queer turns given to things. You never knew where he would take you next; and all the while there seemed to be an odd logical sequence, almost impelling your assent to most unexpected conclusions."[192]

No one questions that Carroll was fundamentally shy, but that he became increasingly withdrawn and depressed as the years passed by, that he was eccentric, and that he lived as a near recluse towards the end of his life. He had begun as a young academic, hopeful and social, giving dinner parties in his room,[193] and entertaining friends and family with jokes, and silly voices, and magic lantern shows. He had given sermons in front of large audiences that went well despite his hesitations of speech. And yet, after he passed away, they couldn't stop talking about the schism in his personality, and about the ways in which he was very different than you might think him to be if you knew him only as the author of *Alice*. (In this they were contradicted by the extremely small circle who knew him well who insisted he was just so.) In a spirit decidedly against the prevailing "speak no ill of the dead" spirit of the times, unflattering portraits were painted of his later years, not by his official biographers, who adored him, but by others. How could this man, beloved to the world, be described as having a "grave, repellent face"? . . . Why would people say, after he had gone, that he was "not an alluring

---

[192] Tollemache, L. A. 1838-1919. (1908). *Old and odd memories.* London: E. Arnold, pp. 308-309, a quote attributed to a friend of Dodgson's.

[193] "For many years he kept in his exhaustive diary the particulars of all the dinner parties he gave—menus and lists of guests, with diagrams showing the positions they occupied at table. He did this to avoid the embarrassment of inviting the same people to meet the same people and partake of the same food twice in succession." *The Lantern.* Vol 3 (March 1917 to March 1918) San Francisco, O'Day, E. F., *The Father of Alice pp 18-25*

personage"? That he was "austere," "self-conscious," "nervous, highly strung", that he was "the stillest and shyest full-grown man I have ever met," that he had a "shyness that made him nervous in the presence of strangers" and which "cut him off while living from all except . . . little girls"? Why would they publish letters in which Carroll's serious work was mocked as deserving of "psychical study?" Why would they stoop to say that he was "a personality apart" and that he "struck discords in the frank harmonious camaraderie of College life?"[194]

Harry Furniss, the man who illustrated Lewis Carroll's last major works of fiction, was one of these voices. He had come to believe that Carroll was crazy, and a few years after Carroll died, he published an unflattering tell-all of his experience working with Carroll. "I was willful and erratic, bordering on insanity," Furniss' account began, "we therefore got on splendidly." Furniss gave three examples to illustrate Carroll's bizarrely excessive requests, the first of which was that Carroll directed Furniss to compose a face using a combination of features taken from many different living individuals ("He invited me to visit friends of his, and strangers too, from John o'Groats to Land's End, so as to collect fragments of faces."). The second example which Furniss gave of Carroll's eccentricity was that, in a concern for secrecy, Carroll had "cut his MS into horizontal strips of four or five lines, then placed the whole of it in a sack and shook it up; taking out piece by piece, he pasted the strips down as they happened to come. . .

---

[194] Tuckwell, W. (1900). *Reminiscences of Oxford.* London [etc.]: Cassell and company. pp 127, 160-161; Paine, A. Bigelow. (1935). *Mark Twain, a biography: the personal and literary life of Samuel Langhorne Clemens.* Twelfth edition New York: Harper & brothers; Bowman, I. (1899). *The story of Lewis Carroll.* London: J.M. Dent & Co.., pp 13-17; Carroll, L. (1907). *Feeding the mind.* London: Chatto & Windus., prefatory note by William H. Draper, p v; Holland, H. Scott. (1919). *A forty years' friendship: letters from the late Henry Scott Holland to Mrs. Drew.* New York: D. Appleton and Co., pp 69, 79-80

. These incongruous strips were elaborately and mysteriously marked with numbers and letters and various hieroglyphics, to decipher which would really have turned my assumed eccentricities into positive madness!"[195]   The third example was Carroll's request, which we have already seen, that Furniss *"draw the last picture first, & work backwards."*   Furniss included the excerpt to show that the letter was annotated (5) 49874 to denote that it was the 5th page of Carroll's 49, 874th letter. [196]   (At his death it was found that Carroll had indexed and catalogued 98,721.[197])   Furniss did not comment on the peculiarity of the request that he illustrate in reverse order, as, although strange, it was undoubtedly not as much of an inconvenience to him as the other requests had been, although his selection of this particular piece of correspondence is suggestive of his general impression— for where a cogent argument can be made in favor of writing backwards as a *plotting* device, it is difficult to see how it could apply to the *illustrations.*   Furniss, who admitted that he pretended to great eccentricities as a part of his artists' "persona", wrote that it was difficult putting up with Carroll's eccentricities, "real ones, not sham like mine." I treated him as a problem," concluded Furniss, "and I solved him."

It had all began innocently enough when, on March 1st, 1885, Lewis Carroll wrote in his diary that he had sent a letter to Harry Furniss, "a very clever illustrator in Punch, asking if he is open to proposals to draw pictures for me."[198]   Furniss, had been just a boy when the *Alice* books came out, and it had been his dream to draw for Carroll someday, but he was bitterly disappointed by the

---

[195] Ibid, p 105

[196] Ibid, p 112

[197] O'Day, E. F. Bonnet, T., (1917) *The Lantern Vol 3* No. 9, The Father of Alice, p 21.

[198] Collingwood, S. Dodgson. (1899). *The life and letters of Lewis Carroll (Rev. C.L. Dodgson).* New York: The Century Co.., p236

disjointed and moralistic subject matter of the Carroll's later novels. Carroll's ability to deal with the world on its own terms continued to disintegrate, with Furniss reporting a distinct change between the years 1890 and 1894, at the beginning of which Carroll had solicited him to provide 'keys' and 'ciphers' to two political illustrations Furniss had done for *Punch* so that Carroll could label the *Punch* taken and bound in the Christ Church Common room. "The simplest way," Carroll had written, "would be for you to put numbers on the faces, and send a list of names numbered to correspond." And yet, only a few years later, Carroll had sent him a letter which read,

> *No doubt it is by your direction that three numbers of your new periodical have come to me. With many thanks for your kind thought, I will beg you not to waste your bounties on so unfit a recipient, for I have neither time nor taste for any such literature. I have more work yet to do than I am likely to have life to do it in—and my taste for comic papers is defunct. We take in Punch in our Common Room, but I never look at it!*

"Hardly a generous remark to make to a *Punch* man who had illustrated two of his books" Furniss concluded, "but this is a bygone."[199] It was a startling change for a man who had sought out not one, but two *Punch* illustrators, and who had been a lifelong devotee of comic writing, but Carroll had his full share of moments of depression in his later years, his nephew admitted, "when old age seemed to mock him with all its futility and feebleness".[200] As we have already discussed, his nervousness had increased, and although he had always been very healthy, he

---

[199] Furniss, H. (1902). *The confessions of a caricaturist.* New York: Harper & brothers., p 272

[200] Collingwood, S. Dodgson. (1899). *The life and letters of Lewis Carroll (Rev. C.L. Dodgson).* New York: The Century Co.., p 363

began to be plagued with a variety of health complaints. He began to be troubled by pain in his knees, first one and then the other, which doctors informed him indicated a constitutional disorder "probably rheumatic in nature." This may have been the reason he "always seemed a little unsteady in his gait" in his later years.[201] He had trouble with the sight in his right eye, recurring respiratory illnesses, migraine headaches, blind spots, multiple hallucinations of moving geometrical patterns referred to as "moving fortifications," and epileptiform seizures.

What happened to Lewis Carroll? Doctors have speculated that his migraine and seizure disorders may have influenced some of the more bizarre aspects of size and shape changes in his *Alice* books, without apparent reference to the fact that these disorders had not yet manifested at this time in Carroll's life.[202] No doctor that I am aware of has speculated about Carroll's awareness of his own increasingly abnormal mental state as evidenced in his fiction. And yet, within each piece there is some harmless Carroll-like character who either speaks in strange riddling ways, or who discusses some form of madness, usually in dreams or half-dreams, or dream like states, from the deluded narrator of *Novelty and Romancement*, to the Mad Hatter of *Alice's Adventures in Wonderland*, to the White Knight of *Through the Looking Glass* (with the setting sun shining so brightly off of his armor, and his "L" shaped moves), to characters which we haven't met yet, De Ciel (Of the Heavens), and the Man in the Moon Professor of *Sylvie and Bruno*. The heavens, the moon, the night, and madness have a common underlying thread, and it was one which Carroll repeatedly wove into his stories—that of

---

[201] Bowman, I. (1899). *The story of Lewis Carroll.* London: J.M. Dent & Co., p 9
[202] The Alice in Wonderland syndrome, Fine EJ., Prog Brain Res. 2013;206:143-5; Alice in Wonderland Syndrome: somesthetic vs visual perceptual disturbance, Lanska JR, Lanska DJ., Neurology. 2013 Mar 26;80(13):1262-4.

lunacy. Our modern terms lunar and lunacy, lunar, meaning of, or pertaining to, the moon, and lunacy, are both derived from Luna, the Roman name for the moon—because it was once believed that the moon played a role in the course of madness. It was a theory which acknowledged the coming and going of sanity.[203] Carroll would compare the changeable nature of lunatics to the phases of the moon a lot in his later books, having his characters say such things as, "like the fickle Moon, my guardian satellite, I change as I go on."[204]

Whereas today there is a growing consensus that mental illness is fundamentally a biological problem involving brain circuits that influence patterns of cognition, emotion and behavior,[205] in the 1800s they were still trying to define madness itself. There had been a troubling increase in the rate of insanity in the general population, which the people believed had been brought on by the increasing pressures of a civilized world. The experts told them that those with a disordered mind were suffering from a failure to make sense of the input received from the exterior world, and most specifically that they were unable to ignore the irrelevant connections which those with more healthy minds would filter out. The problem, more precisely, was that the *foundation* of the madman's reasoning was compromised by the incorporation of incorrect underlying premises, incoherent ideas cemented together, faulty keystones that could not sustain their walls. The mad had not lost their ability to reason, wrote the

---

[203] Tuke, D. Hack. (1882). *Chapters on the history of the insane in the British isles.* London: K. Paul, Trench & co.., p. 9 ("Those are called lunatics whose attacks are exacerbated every month when the moon is full.")

[204] This statement was made by the lunatic architect in Carroll's *Vision of the Three T's.* Carroll, L. (1874). *Notes by an Oxford chiel.* Oxford:: James Parker and Co.

[205] Aldhouse, Peter, and Andy Coghlan. "A revolution in mental health." *New Scientist* 11 May 2013: 8-9. Print.

philosopher John Locke, they reasoned correctly *but for* the acceptance of these incorrect underlying premises.

Madmen do not appear to me to have lost the faculty of reasoning; but having joined together some ideas very wrongly, they mistake them for truths, and they err as men do that argue right from wrong principles. For by the violence of their imaginations, having taken their fancies for realities, they make right deductions from them. Thus you shall find a distracted man fancying himself a king, with a right inference require suitable attendance, respect and obedience: others, who have thought themselves made of glass, have used the caution necessary to preserve such brittle bodies. Hence it comes to pass that a man, who is very sober, and of a right understanding in all other things, may in one particular be as frantic as any in Bedlam; if either by any very strong impression, or long fixing his fancy upon one sort of thoughts, incoherent ideas have been cemented together so powerfully, as to remain united.[206]

Locke's ideas were quoted repeatedly, and especially his example of the otherwise rational lunatic who believes he is made of glass. There were, in actuality, many living in lunatic asylums who thought just that, but one of the first men made of glass was fictional, and appeared in Cervantes story, "El Licienciado Vidriera", which translates roughly to "The Educated Man of Glass", and which appeared in translation in England in 1835 as "The Rational Lunatic of Salamanca." Cervantes story was about a man who had been given a drug mixed into a quince by a woman who had bought the drug as a love potion. The drug caused the man's hands and feet to shake, and he became delirious. He was kept in bed under treatment for 6 months, a time in which he was reduced almost to a skeleton, and, although he eventually

---

[206] Locke, J. (1823). *The works of John Locke.* A new edition, London: Printed for T. Tegg, pp 150-151

recovered his bodily health, his mind remained affected, so that he imagined that he was made entirely of glass. Strangely, his mind was clearer and quicker than ever, something which he believed was attributable to the fact that, "glass being of a subtler and more delicate substance the mind would operate through it more quickly and efficaciously than through the gross and earthly body."

In Cervantes' story, the man made of glass was brought to the University as a curiosity, and the professors of medicine and philosophy were astounded to find that a person so mad had so good an understanding as to answer every question so intelligently.[207]   Unsurprisingly, perhaps, as tremor, delirium, anorexia, intensified thought and insanity are all symptoms of severe mercury poisoning, a little research reveals that mercury often played a role in ancient love potions and philters.[208]

As a result of Locke's definition, the term "rational lunatic" began to enter everyday speech, where it was defined in the common press as "the best definition of an eccentric," and someone "too lunatic to be at large, too rational to be confined."[209] Everyone had encountered an eccentric whose derangement did not prevent the fulfillment of other duties. One doctor gave the example of a judge who believed that he was a turtle, writing, "This ridiculous impression did not prevent him from sitting on the bench, and fulfilling his judicial functions as regularly as his

---

[207] *The parterre.* Vol 2 (1835) [London: E. Wilson.. pp 155-156
[208] Wedeck, H. Ezekiel. (1963). *Love potions through the ages: a study of amatory devices and mores.* New York: Citadel Press., p288; Massengill, S. Evans. (1943). *A sketch of medicine and pharmacy and a view of its progress by the Massengill family from the fifteenth to the twentieth century.* [Bristol, Tenn.: The S. E. Massengill company. P 364
[209]*The Universal magazine, New Series.* Vol 6 (1806) London: H. D. Symonds, p 499; *The Mirror of literature, amusement, and instruction.* Vol 34 (1839) London, J. Limbird, p 296; *Frank Leslie's monthly.* Vol 7 No.s 1-6 (1860-1863) New York, N.Y.: F. Leslie., p 221

learned colleagues."[210]   Trying to determine when confinement was necessary was therefore a difficult call for a lunacy doctor to make. It was difficult to determine the point at which eccentricity became lunacy, and lunacy inquiries were all the more complicated because the insane often retained enough presence of mind to try to hide their nonconventional beliefs. It might take some careful questioning to uncover that the man walking strangely was doing so because he believed that the floor was burning him—if he still retained enough presence of mind to know how his belief would be perceived. As one of Carroll's characters would say in trying to explain why he could not confess that the words he had spoken were not his own, "I had not the moral courage to make such a confession. The character of a 'lunatic' is not, I believe, very difficult to *acquire*; but it is amazingly difficult to *get rid of*; and it seemed quite certain that any such speech as that would quite justify the issue of a writ '*de lunatic inquirendo*.'"[211]

A man's ability to control the rise and succession of his thoughts is a measure of his sanity, in a sliding scale, from the steadfast who have such a control over the associating process as to admit into conscious thought only those ideas which fit in with their conception of rational life, to those who actively seek out unusual associations in the pursuit of originality, such as our poets, comedians, and our geniuses. A little further along on the scale, original thinking becomes eccentricity as we let go, and allow ourselves to entertain unbidden ideas that we know are strange, because it is not worth resisting. When we no longer *can*

[210] Millingen, J. G. 1782-1862. (1842). *Aphorisms on the treatment and management of the insane: with considerations on public and private lunatic asylums, pointing out the errors in the present system.* Philadelphia: E. Barrington & G.D. Haswell., p 27
[211] Carroll, L. (1893). *Sylvie and Bruno concluded.* London: Macmillan and Co., p 130.

resist an increasing current of irrational ideas—that is madness. In this madness, odd associations can assume a morbidly vivid importance in the brain, the classic fixed idea, such as the man who believes he is made of glass, or they can assume the form of outright hallucination, the intrusion of dream elements into waking life.

In 1865, the year *Alice* was published, and in the several years after, during which Lewis Carroll saw his greatest literary success; he had not yet earned the reputation for rigidity and eccentricity that he would later have. He was working hard, and thinking fast and furiously, working in exhausting paroxysms which might keep him up until 4 in the morning. He was living through a time of sweeping changes in the way Universities were run, including the passage of a series of enactments which would potentially affect his academic position at the University.[212] When Carroll began his career at Oxford, it had been a position which was considered to be for life on the condition that he remain unmarried and proceed to Holy Orders, and the work required of him was largely left to his own discretion. While Carroll remained largely unaffected by these changes throughout his lifetime, this threat to his lifestyle engendered a distress and agitation which would drive him to write a series of works so dense in their allusions that they reached a point of nearly inaccessible genius—short pieces intended for adult readers, dealing mainly with in-university politics taking place at Oxford University—published not under the names Charles Dodgson or Lewis Carroll, but anonymously. The first 3 were "The evaluation of π, *The Dynamics of a Parti-cle*, and *Facts, Figures and Fancies*. Although they apparently referred to mathematical formulae, they were *not* about mathematics, but

---

[212] *The Living age.* Sixth Series, Vol 18, (April, May June 1898) Boston: The Living Age Company, p. 18

about social controversies with references "obscure" even to the general public of the time. His nephew wrote later that, "It may not be possible in all instances to explain an allusion, where it is evident that an allusion was made."[213] Those who *did* understand complimented the pieces on their "startling ingenuity," and called them "unsurpassable" and "sly." And it is no wonder they were found to be so obscure, as they required not only an understanding of Oxonian politics, but also of mathematics and literary works. The second set of three writings dealt chiefly with Carroll's unhappiness over artistically questionable architectural changes made to Tom Quad Square where Carroll lived. Authorship of the first, *The New Belfry*, was attributed to D. C. L., a transposition of Carroll's initials (C. D. L.), while the next two, *The Vision of the Three T's*, and *The Blank Cheque*, were attributed simply to "the author of *The New Belfry*."

Why D. C. L.? The letters D C L are Carroll's initials, appearing backwards, as they might in a roster listing names, last name first, followed by the first and middle names, Charles Lutwidge Dodgson C L D, as Dodgson, Charles Lutwidge D,C L, or, phonetically, De Ciel which translates (from Spanish to English) to "of the heavens." A character named Mr. De Ciel appears in the last piece of the set (the apparently straight forward *The Blank Cheque* [214]) as a man visiting a friend who is relating why she will be letting her maid direct her summer vacation plans. One

---

[213] Carroll, L. (1899). *The Lewis Carroll picture book: a selection from the unpublished writings and drawings of Lewis Carroll : together with reprints from scarce and unacknowledged work.* London: T.F. Unwin., p 98

[214] Apparently, but never the case in Carroll's works. Carroll's nephew identifies the friend, Mrs. Nivers, as the University, and her several boys as various key players in University politics. Carroll, L. (1899). *The Lewis Carroll picture book: a selection from the unpublished writings and drawings of Lewis Carroll: together with reprints from scarce and unacknowledged work.* London: T.F. Unwin., pp 147-148

statement which perhaps stood out as somewhat too extreme for the context was De Ciel's plaintive deliberation, "One of us is dreaming, no doubt, . . . or—or perhaps I'm going mad."

In reality, although the story worked on its own in a surreal but charming way, the entire fable was based on arrangements made for the building of new schools. De Ciel's friend, Mrs. Nivers, represented Oxford University, the maid, the committee appointed to select a plan, and her three boys, various players involved in the scheme.[215] At one point earlier in his life Carroll had written a poem in which a young woman complained at her reluctant beau, "You'll find no one, like me, who can manage to see Your meaning, you talk so obscurely." Authorship of the poem was attributed to B. B.[216] Who knows why? There may be some connection to Carroll's later *Hunting of the Snark*, in which the names of the crew members involved in the hunt all began with the letter B. Again, who knows why? Why would he later write under the initial K? At the conclusion of *The Blank Cheque*, at any rate, Carroll took pains to include a "moral" to make sure that he was understood. "Everything," Carroll wrote, "has a moral if you choose to look for it."[217] And, at the end of the day, that is how most people now feel about Carroll's books, that he means *something* by the things he has written, but that we just don't know *what*. As one author wrote, "His Wonderland is a country populated by insane mathematicians. We feel the whole is an escape into a world of masquerade; we feel that if we could pierce their disguises, we might discover that Humpty Dumpty and the March Hare were Professors and Doctors of Divinity

---

[215] Carroll, L. (1899). *The Lewis Carroll picture book: a selection from the unpublished writings and drawings of Lewis Carroll : together with reprints from scarce and unacknowledged work.* London: T.F. Unwin., pp 147-148

[216] *College rhyme Vol 3* (1862) Oxford: T. & G. Shrimpton, Cambridge, MacMillan & Co., p 11

[217] Carroll, L. (1874). *Notes by an Oxford chiel.* Oxford:: James Parker and Co.

enjoying a mental holiday."[218] Who could tell if a man so brilliant, and so intentionally obscure, were to stop making sense? But it did happen, somewhere along the line, as you will soon see.

What happened to Lewis Carroll?

There are two strong possibilities.

---

[218] Chesterton, G. K. (1911). *A defence of nonsense: and other essays.* New York: Dodd, Mead & company, p 5

The Magic Cupboard

Imagine his surprise, when he took the spoilt plate from the cupboard, to find an exquisite picture upon it. Doubtless he questioned whether he was waking or dreaming; it was too like a fairy tale.

-Charles R. Gibson, The Marvels of Photography

In the sixteenth century, an Italian Philosopher-Scientist by the name of Battista Porta shuttered the window of his room so tightly that absolutely no light could enter except by way of a small hole, no bigger than the dimension of his smallest finger, which he had cut in the center of the shutter. In so doing, Porta caused an inverted image of the scene outside his window to be displayed on the opposite wall. Porta invited crowds to see his "pictures painted by light."[219] Over the years, it was discovered that a glass lens at the hole in the shutter would sharpen the image, and a mirror, or looking glass, would be placed close to the lens to re-orient the image so that it no longer appeared to be upside down. The wealthy began to construct these dark chambers, or camera obscuras, in their homes as a source of novelty and amusement. For many years, men applied themselves to trying to permanently "fix" the image of the camera obscura using chemicals known to react to light. It was the beginning of photography, the camera obscura, exposure of a sensitized plate, and developing and fixing the image by chemical processes. Producing a negative image off of which pcitures would be printed on paper would come later.

---

[219] Gibson, C. R. (1919). *The marvels of photography: describing its discovery & many of its achievements.* London: Seeley, Service & Co. Limited, p 15

The first man to obtain a permanent "photograph" was the Frenchman Joseph Nicephore Niépce, in the early 1800s. Niépce had created a small camera obscura using a box and the lens of a solar microscope which had belonged to his grandfather. He then placed a tin plate coated with a form of light-sensitive asphalt, called bitumen, inside the camera and exposed the plate to the light for several hours, after which he used a chemical solvent to wash away the bitumen which had been *unaffected* by the light, thereby producing an etched silhouette which he called a heliograph.

In 1829, Niépce entered into a partnership with the artist and business man Jean Jaques Claude Daguerre. Daguerre had made a name for himself by the creation of giant movable landscape paintings, which he called dioramas. He had often used the camera obscura to trace reflected images in the creation of his landscapes, and, as so many others had before him, he dreamt of fixing the images permanently. Daguerre avidly followed the status of experiments in the art, but he learned of Niépce only by chance, through an optician whom they both worked with to obtain the lenses for their camera obscuras. Daguerre pursued Niépce until a partnership was formed in which both men agreed to share information on their ongoing experiments with different chemicals and processes. Niépce died suddenly of congestion of the brain on July 5, 1833, due perhaps to the chemicals with which he had been working so intensively, for Niépce and Daguerre had made a tremendous discovery which dramatically shortened the exposure time required to make a fixed image.

According to Daguerre, *he* had made the discovery and by chance alone. He had placed an inadequately exposed plate showing no image into a storage cupboard with the intention of cleaning the surface for reuse the next day. When he took the plate out the next morning, he found a distinct and perfect picture. *"Another prepared plate was quickly exposed for an equally short time within the camera, and again a sojourn of twenty-four hours within the magic cupboard sufficed to bring out a picture."*[220] By process of long elimination, the effect was traced to an open dish of liquid mercury. The vapour produced by the mercury within the closed cupboard had been sufficient to cause a chemical reaction on the photographic plate. By heating the mercury, and thereby increasing the amount of vapour produced, the effect could be achieved much more quickly.

Daguerre worked with Niépce's son to sign a new agreement, and the two men opened their business to investors on March 15, 1838, but without success. The use of mercury in image development may have been a fantastic discovery, but the process could not be protected by a patent. Once the secret was known, anyone could make use of it. Unable to make a profitable business of his discovery, and confronted with H. W. Fox Talbot's announcement of his own new process in early 1839, Daguerre announced the secret of the "Daguerrotype" to the world.

Talbot's process, in which an image was fixed first as a negative image, would eventually form the basis of modern photography, but not until later improvements in image quality and exposure time. Talbot's pictures were "mere shadows," requiring an exposure of an hour or more in bright sunshine, whereas the daguerreotype produced a far better image and required only twenty minutes of exposure. It was no contest. Although it was unwieldy and technically difficult, the Daguerrotype process dominated the art of photography from 1839 to 1851 because it produced a better image.

---

[220] The Photographic Times (1887), Vol XVII Friday, January 7, 1887, New York: Scovill Manufacturing Company, Chapters in the History of Photography. Chapter II. By W. Jerome Harrison pp 7-9

The next transformative improvement in photograph was made by Frederick Scott Archer in 1851. Archer's process built upon Talbot's, and involved the use of a gel collodion solution on glass photographic plates and produced a better image with less difficulty and a faster exposure time than the Daguerrotype. It had been only 12 years since Daguerre and Talbot had announced that they could fix the images of the camera obscura, and in that time, the exposure time of the daguerreotype had been reduced to a fraction of a minute, but Archer's collodion process had enough advantages to it that it was taking over. The collodion process not only quickly displaced the daguerreotype, it resulted in an explosive increase in the number of people practicing the art. In 1851, there were only fifty-one professional photographers in England, and by 1881, there were 7,614. Archer's wet-plate collodion was the primary process in use in photography from 1851 until 1894.[221] It was within these years, the years which bracketed the majority of Charles Dodgson's adult life, that we are most concerned.

Charles Dodgson was first introduced to the art of photography in 1855 by his Uncle Skeffington, who was influenced, in part, no doubt, by his close business association with Dr. Hugh Diamond, with whom he served on the lunacy commission. Diamond had been so active in publicizing new advances in photography and in doing so, making the art more accessible to the public, that he had been honored for his efforts.[222] Diamond was using photography in his treatment of inmates at the Surrey Lunatic Asylum, and he had presented photographs of "the types of insanity" in the" first exhibition of pictures produced

---

[221] Gibson, C. R. 1870-1931. (1919). *The marvels of photography: describing its discovery & many of its achievements.* London: Seeley, Service & co., limited.
[222] English Mechanic and World of Science: No. 1,111 vol 43, Mar-Aug 1886, July 9, 1886, Scientific News, p 413 London: E. J. Kibblewhite

by the agency of solar radiation" held at the Great Exhibition of 1851. He would later present the photographs again in an exhibition in Paris, after which one reviewer would write,

I have before me a collection of fourteen portraits of women of various ages. Some are smiling, others appear to be dreaming. All have something strange in their physiognomy; that is what one sees at first glance. If one ponders them for a longer period of time, one grows sad against one's will. All these faces have an unusual expression which causes pain in the observer.

Of particular interest were the photographs taken over time, the "contracted" features of a woman "deformed through suffering" taken on admission, as compared to those taken on recovery. This was what Diamond wanted others in his field to notice, that you could *see* madness—that there was a physical component to insanity that those in the field should strive to understand.[223]

In January of 1856 Dodgson and his friend Robert Southey were intending to spend the day in photography, but they went instead to visit Diamond, who gave Dodgson a photograph of his uncle and one of a student at Oxford's Kings college.[224] It was less than a week later that Dodgson decided to obtain his own photographic equipment. We can only imagine what they spoke about and the ways in which it influenced Dodgson. Dodgson would become well-known for his photographs of young girls. Had it occurred to Dodgson then that if Diamond could use photography in an entirely new way, to reveal the physically

---

[223] Gilman, S. L., (1977) The Face of Madness, Hugh Diamond and the Origin of Psychiatric Photography, New Jersey: The Citadel Press, pp 7-16; The Photographic Art Journal, Vol 5, 1853, New York: W. B. Smith, London: Trubner & Co., pp 155-160

[224] Wakeling, E. (2001) *Lewis Carroll's Diaries, The Private Journals of Charles Lutwidge Dodgson*, Vol. 2 January to December 1854, p 24 and note 45.

visible manifestations of degraded mental states, that *he* might be able to use it reveal the physical expression of innocence and purity? If pondering mental ruin could cause one to grow sad, wouldn't pondering innocence cause one to grow happy? Dodgson was looking for the "big idea" of his life. It was only days after this meeting, in fact, that Dodgson began writing his story *Novelty and Romancement*, the story in which he wrote, "I had dreamed at night that the great idea of my life was to be fulfilled".[225]

In the abandoned Daguerrotype process, photographic plates were placed in a heated mercury bath, usually for a period of 2 minutes. It was an art form, with as many variations in temperature, time of exposure and quantity of mercury as there were photographers. A (dangerous) hint from the American Hand Book of the Daguerrotype: "Keep the mercury hot." The use of mercury vapour in photographic development was no longer required with the advent of the collodion process, but it would be a mistake to believe that the use of mercury was altogether abandoned. Bichloride of mercury, or corrosive sublimate, was used to a considerable extent to darken or intensify negatives, both on paper and on glass.[226]

Bichloride of mercury is the same compound which had been used so aggressively by physicians in the early 1800s in the treatment of disease, that same substance which was found too toxic for most uses and transformed chemically into the less poisonous, but still quite toxic calomel. Physicians had found, in fact, that they tended to wind up with mercury poisoning themselves if they spent too much time applying mercurial

---

[225] Ibid, P 26

[226] On the Employment of Bichloride of Mercury (Corrosive Sublimate) with paper Photographs. M Disderi, from La Lumiere, September 24, 1853, p170 The Journal of the Photographic Society of London, vol. 1, (1853-1854) London: Taylor and Francis

ointments containing bichloride of mercury to their patients, as the chemical would make its way through their leather gloves and into their own skin. This problem was solved by directing patients to apply their own salves, a solution which the doctors of the time thought benefited the patient as much by increasing their constitutional exposure as it benefited the doctors by decreasing theirs. There wasn't much warning about the danger of bichloride of mercury in photography in the early days. People then were so much more accustomed to the presence and purportedly beneficial use of mercury in all its forms that the danger could not be fully appreciated.

Over the years, however, the dangers of bichloride of mercury would become more well known, so that in a 1913 issue of *Camera, a Practical Magazine for Photographers*, the authors warned that bichloride of mercury absorbed through the skin could have fatal results, and that "This chemical is a good thing to leave alone, except when required for photographic intensification."

Poisoning in this case takes place by absorption, acting through an unbroken skin and producing nearly all the terrible effects of taking the poison internally. When this salt is taken internally, the first effect is a coppery, rank metallic taste and burning sensation of the mouth and throat; great difficulty in swallowing is experienced, vomiting occurs, the lips sometimes become much swollen and very tender, the mucous membrane of the lips and tongue have a whitened aspect, cramps in the legs and purging, sometimes delirium and salivation, but this latter distressing symptom does not always occur. The symptoms here described are only a few that take place in bichloride of mercury poisoning.[227]

---

[227] Columbia Photographic Society, P. *Camera: a practical magazine for photographers*. Philadelphia: Columbia Photographic Society, pp 536-538

The exceptionally poisonous bichloride of mercury was good for the intensification of wet plate negatives, an act which could be performed either after the final washing, or after drying if the negative was first remoistened with water.   One early photographer reported in 1863 that "Many of my negatives were taken in Italy, and brought home, after fixing, for the intensification to be done in England."—a process which was accomplished by varnishing the edge of the plates, moistening the film with distilled water, then pouring on a saturated solution of bichloride of mercury, which is "poured off as soon as the film has taken the proper colour".[228] Bichloride of mercury was also good for strengthening an image for the purposes of enlargement ("take one drachm of a saturated solution of bichloride of mercury to ten ounces of water and pour on and off the plate till the image is of a rich blue-black"), and for saving old prints.[229] Some photographers used bichloride of mercury to improve the tone of blacks by *pre*-treating their plates. There were so many possible uses. Bichloride of mercury found its way, even, into the composition of the "best and most durable" paste for mounting positives, and as a good way to remove silver stains from a photographer's clothing and fingers.[230]

---

[228] Royal Photographic Society of Great Britain. *The Photographic Journal.* London, vol 8 Feb 16, 1863 The Photographic Journal, Lieut.-Col. Stuart Wortley P221

[229] Wilson, Edward Livingston, 1838-1903, and Mathew Carey Lea. *Photographic Mosaics: an Annual Record of Photographic Progress.* Philadelphia, [etc.]: Benerman & Wilson [etc.], 1885-1886 vol 37, pp 13-14, 35, 53

[230] Humphrey, S. D. 1823-1883. *A Practical Manual of the Collodion Process: Giving In Detail a Method for Producing Positive And Negative Pictures On Glass And Paper. Ambrotypes. Printing Process ...* 3d ed., rev. and greatly enl. New York: Humphrey's journal print, 1857, pp 8, 200; Hepworth, T. Cradock., Crookes, W. *The Photographic news for amateur photographer* v. 2 (Mar. 11 - Sept. 2, 1859) London: Cassell, Petter, and Galpin, p 48 "A correspondent, "Raven" has informed us that he has found, from experience, that the best

It was also possible to create a more intense and vibrant photograph by using bichloride of mercury to change a positive *back into a negative* which might then be *again* intensified, in as many iterations as the photographer might wish.

After fixing and well washing the positive, pour over it a solution of bi-chloride of mercury. This will bleach the picture and convert the silver image into one composed of chloride of mercury (calomel), chloride of silver, and perhaps a little black oxide of mercury. This image, when viewed by transmitted light, is more intense than before; but its intensity may be greatly increased by first washing it thoroughly, and then pouring over it a weak solution of sulphide of ammonium, which forms black sulphide of mercury.

With a portrait lens of 4-ins. Or 5-ins. focus, a half inch stop between the lenses, and the sensitive process which we have described, an instantaneous positive may be taken of objects out-of-doors tolerably well lighted,and the details of the shadows fully brought out. This positive may then be intensified into a negative by means of bi-chloride of mercury..."[231]

The process of using mercury to intensify photographic negatives captured the mind of the young Charles Dodgson. He imagined the possibility of intensifying an author's writings in the same way, a subject which he dealt with in his 1856 story, *Photography Extraordinary*, which began,

---

thing to remove stains from the fingers is bichloride of mercury dissolved in warm water; dip the fingers in, and the stains disappear by rubbing."
[231] Sutton, T. *Photographic notes.* Vol 1-3 (1856) London: Sampson Low, Son & Co., p 289

The recent extraordinary discovery in Photography, as applied to the operations of the mind, has reduced the art of novel writing to the merest mechanical labour. We have been kindly permitted by the artist to be present during one of his experiments; but as the invention has not yet been given to the world, we are only at liberty to relate the results, suppressing all details of chemicals and manipulation." The operator began by stating that the ideas of the feeblest intellect, when once received on properly prepared paper, could be "developed" up to any required degree of intensity.[232]

To prove the machine, the operator calls in a young man "of the very weakest possible physical and mental powers." After a "mesmeric rapport" is established between the machine and the young man, a mild story develops, full of soft imagery such as light drops of rain, a pony moving gracefully, a calm smile, languid eyes, and gentle regrets of lost love. The observers announce that it belongs "to the milk-and-water School of Novels." The novel is then dipped into a chemical bath, which intensifies its dramatic action and imagery. One more round of intensification is then performed, which transforms the story to the highest possible degree, to the "Spasmodic or German School" of literature. The intensified novel now includes a wildly tempestuous night and a headlong rush down a precipitous mountain gorge. The pony is now a horse bounding at a mad gallop, and the rider's face, his "knotted brows—rolling eyeballs—and clenched teeth" express the intense agony of his mind, and the weird visions looming upon his burning brain.

---

[232] Carroll, L. (1899). *The Lewis Carroll picture book: a selection from the unpublished writings and drawings of Lewis Carroll : together with reprints from scarce and unacknowledged work.* London: T.F. Unwin., pp 28-32

Photography Extraordinary is an allegory for the development and intensification of a photographic negative. That is the intentional allegory, but what is truly amazing is Dodgson's grasp, which *must* have been unintentional, of the way in which the action of mercury intensifies the thought processes of the *mind*, creating an exaggeration of emotions, thoughts coming quickly like a storm of lightening, excessive interpersonal sensitivity, reactions out of proportion to the underlying emotional stimuli, deeper depressions and hotter anger. A novel written by a man whose mind had been intensified by mercury would be much more likely to be intense and dramatic, out of proportion, wild and mad.

Between the years 1857 and 1862, Charles Dodgson created almost 1,000 negatives.[233] In the years that followed he produced many, many more. He kept them in cupboards in the studio he had constructed on the roof above his suite of rooms. "He also used the studio to renumber and organize his vast collection of negatives, collate his albums, and make new prints when needed."

Mercuric Chloride is extremely toxic. Exposure to it, by ingestion or absorption, can cause serious damage to the gastrointestinal tract and the renal system. It is formed by the union of metallic mercury and chlorine, and when it decomposes, as happens over time or on exposure to heat or sunlight, it can revert to those forms, emitting highly toxic chloride and mercury fumes.[234] Mercury has the strange ability to easily change form. Elemental mercury is poorly absorbed by the gastrointestinal tract and cannot pass the blood-brain barrier, but in *gaseous* form, it is almost completely absorbed through the respiratory tract, and

---

[233] Nidel, D. R. (2002) *Dreaming in Pictures, the Photography of Lewis Carroll.* New Haven and London: Yale University Press., p 17
[234] http://www.cameochemicals.noaa.gov/chemical/3828, 2/27/14

rapidly crosses the blood-brain barrier to cause the neurotoxicity which is more commonly known as *mad hatter's disease*. On a cellular level—in the body as a whole—the dissolved vapor is oxidized to Hg2+ which causes nephrotoxity, damaging the kidneys as it passes through them.

The extent to which any one individual can tolerate and excrete the mercury to which they are exposed has to do with a variety of factors, the most basic of which is the purely mechanical issue of how much of the mercury will be retained, and how much of the mercury will be excreted. This most basic factor is *compromised over time* by the mercury to which an individual is exposed, as the damage caused by the mercury as it passes through the kidneys lessens the kidneys' ability to filter toxins from the body. In that way, a low continuous exposure will become an increased exposure *for the individual,* as more of the mercury is retained in the body for greater lengths of time, in the same way that a dripping faucet can begin to fill a sink basin with a clogged drain.

Lewis Carroll was exposed to bichloride of mercury for many years in his work with his photographic negatives. It has been easy to overlook this factor in Lewis Carroll's life, as improvements in photographic equipment have meant that more recent photographers have had much less need to resort to the use of mercury for image intensification. Lewis Carroll's exposure would have reached a crisis point in the years beginning in the summer of 1875 when Carroll discovered that many of his negatives had been damaged and erased by (he speculated) having been kept in shut-up boxes in an unventilated cupboard.[235] He had thousands of negatives at this point, and on opening each

---

[235] Wakeling, E. (2001) *Lewis Carroll's Diaries, The Private Journals of Charles Lutwidge Dodgson*, Vol. 6, April 1868-1876, pp 408-409

shut-up box, he would have been exposed to the dust and fumes of the degraded mercuric chloride trapped within.

So little research has been performed on exposure to degraded mercuric chloride under this set of circumstances, that demonstrating its' probable effect requires the use of analogous cases. Over time, mercuric chloride will degrade back into its original components, mercury and chlorine, in the form of dust and/or vapour. The following case is an example of the destructive influence of mercury inhaled in the form of dust: Powdered mercury, a combination of one part of metallic mercury triturated with two parts of chalk (also called grey powder or hydrargyrum cum creta), was once commonly used in fingerprint photography. This fine powder would be applied liberally to surfaces the perpetrator of a crime might have touched, with the hope that fingerprints might be revealed. In 1949 researchers found that nearly all of the men engaged in fingerprint photography at a Lancashire Constabulary had abnormally high mercury levels as a result of breathing in the mercury dust. One of the men was a 45 year old sergeant who had investigated about 300 crimes a year for a period of three years. During this time period he developed intention tremor, halting and tremulous speech, and deterioration of his fine motor control, so that his handwriting required great concentration. His gums became very tender, and five of his teeth were loose. He reported that he was "a nervous wreck," that giving evidence in court was "becoming a nightmare" and that he could no longer stand still or answer questions without embarrassment. The study authors determined that his symptoms had a direct relationship to the intensity of his exposure.[236] Bichloride of mercury can also

---

[236] Hunter, D. (1962). *The diseases of occupations.* 3rd ed. Boston: Little, Brown, & Co., pp 299-300; Mercury poisoning from fingerprint photography, an occupational hazard of policemen., Agate JN, Buckell, Ind Hyg Newsl. 1949

degrade to mercury vapor within the human body. In an "in vivo" parallel to Lewis Carroll's negative boxes, a recent medical study reported that no autopsy was performed on a man who had committed suicide by ingesting bichloride of mercury "in order to prevent potential inhalation of mercury vapor by pathology staff."[237]

Lewis Carroll continued to have problems with the deterioration of his photographic negatives. 3 years later, in the summer of 1878, he was still trying to find a solution to the damaged and erased negatives. He spent days sorting through the negatives, and had the cupboard moved to his upper bedroom in an effort to keep the negatives from the dampness. Did he attempt to bring the images back to his negatives with baths of bichloride of mercury? Almost certainly. In any event, his actions in moving the negative cupboard, now sporting ventilation holes if his previous plans had been carried out, into his warm dry bedroom would have been a less dramatic—but ongoing—source of exposure.

It was during and after *this time period* that Lewis Carroll's physical, mental and emotional health began to fall apart, and *this period* which has been identified as that in which his literary efforts took a turn for the worse, but it was just the beginning, the start of a *cascade* of emotional and physical problems that Carroll experienced. Was it all due to his exposure to mercury during the course of his photography? It may have been only the initiating factor in a more catastrophic level of exposure, for not long after Carroll began to experience increasingly poor health, he broke away from the harmless homeopathic treatments he had long

---

Dec;9(12):6
[237] Post-mortem CT findings following intentional ingestion of mercuric chloride, Iino M, O'Donnell CJ, Burke MP, Leg Med (Tokyo) 2009 May;11(3):136-8.

been favoring, and began to seek care from the practitioners of traditional medicine.

Widespread Error

"And now, I must take either poison or blue-pill, for things cannot last very long as they are."

-A Romance in Real (Academic) Life (1871)

For many years, Doctors had been prescribing mercury based medications for a tremendous variety of physical and mental illnesses, based on the theory that such illnesses arose from a disordered state of digestion—from the failure of the liver to secrete sufficient bile. So it came as quite a surprise when a set of animal experiments designed to test the theory revealed that not only did mercury have *no* influence in increasing the secretion of bile, when used to the point of salivation or other symptoms of poisoning, it greatly *diminished* secretion. The report was read at a meeting of the British Medical Association held at the Oxford Divinity School on August 7, 1868. The speaker, Dr. J. Hughes Bennet, tried to impress the importance of the results on the Association:

If the refutation of a widespread error be as important as the establishment of a new truth, the practical advantage of demonstrating that mercury is not a cholagogue cannot be too highly estimated. Although in recent times the administration of mercurial for hepatic diseases has greatly diminished, their employment is still very general, and in India almost universal. Recent cases demonstrate that long-continued salivation and great loss of health have been produced in the attempts to remove old abscesses or other chronic diseases of the organs. There are few of its lesions in which it is still not thought advisable to try small or full doses of the drug."[238]

Bennet's report on the failure of mercury to increase the secretion of bile was published early the next year and was reviewed in the monthly medical journal, *The Practitioner*, with the comment, "That podophylline ["called vegetable mercury"[239]], albeit lauded in no measured terms for its flow-of-bile-producing qualities, should prove a traitor, was a blow which some little exertion of moral courage could enable the believer to survive; but that any doubt should be felt about the capabilities of calomel and blue pill, and extractum taraxaci, in "acting upon the liver," must have conveyed a shock in various quarters, from which we should imagine there are many still suffering."[240] The reviewer concluded that the study, which he emphasized had been "conducted by men of proven ability," clearly showed "what careful observation in practice must have taught the unprejudiced," that faith and trust in the bile producing action of mercury had been "as ill-judged as it was strong." Clearly the reviewer had *not* been one of those physicians completely sold on mercurial medications, and he looked forward to the end of the over-identification of the liver as the basis of virtually every complaint.

For a time after Bennet's experiments were published in 1869, doctors turned away from mercury, but they turned back. After an initial shock, they had to ask themselves if it hadn't been the mercury *use* which was in error, but merely the *theory* under which it was employed. It didn't help matters that at virtually the

---

[238] *Medicine in modern times: or, Discourses delivered at a meeting of the British medical association at Oxford.* (1869) London: Macmillan & co., p 235
[239] Ringer, S. (1878). *A handbook of therapeutics.* London: H.K. Lewis, p 413
[240] *The Practitioner, A Monthly Journal of* Therapeutics, Vol II January to June 1869, London: MacMillan and Co., pp 355-358

same point in time another investigation had been performed which would be used to champion the gentleness of low dose mercurials. In the year proceeding Bennet's experiment, a doctor had presented a blackened piece of large intestine before the Pathological Society of London. The specimen was unusually dark in color, but was mottled with lighter colored bumps situated in the sub mucosa so that the appearance of the intestine was similar to that of the skin of a toad. The lighter color was due, the doctor informed the Society, to deposits of mercury, and the intestine had been taken from a woman who had taken a grain of calomel or other mercurial medication every night for the last 43 years of her life. The doctor emphasized that the woman had been of an extraordinarily strong constitution "and probably stood alone as an instance of the daily administration of small doses of mercury for so long a period without having induced salivation, soreness of the gums, necrosis of the bones, or other symptoms which usually follow from a long course of the drug."[241] To be sure, she had suffered some hair raising medical issues before her death, including pain, heart disease, and the partial collapse of her chest ten years before. On autopsy it had been found that her left lung had collapsed and adhered to the chest wall, and her organs were in various states of serious degeneration, *but* she had reached the age of 74, and other physicians present at the meeting seized upon the case to exclaim that "the effects of mercury upon the system were not so deleterious as many Practitioners supposed."[242]

The story made its rounds, and with every reiteration, the degree of the resulting injury the woman had suffered lessened. There was no mention of the blackened intestine harboring its

---

[241] *The Medical times and gazette.* London: John Churchill and Sons, Reports of Societies, July 6, 1867, p 21.
[242] Ibid.

toad-skin bumps of mercury, no mention of the collapsed lung, the dramatically shrunken liver or the gall bladder distended with bile, instead those retelling the story related a degree of fatty degeneration of the heart no more than that to be expected at that age, "without other than good effects apparently," or with "no suffering" at all."[243] Other stories began to be told about this old man, or that old woman who had taken low dose mercurials for decades without harm.   Far from holding these cases of exceptional constitution up as rarities, the doctors of the time used them to justify their own beliefs and practices, albeit maintaining a certain safe conservatism by noting that the patients had taken the pills for such prolonged periods of their "own accord", "whether doctors allowed it or not", and "against medical advice".

Just how widespread this story of harmless long-term blue pill use became can be illustrated by the fact that jokes began to be told in contradiction to it, such as the following comment made by a ranch hand in the United States in the year 1877,

> *I remember a half-witted, faithful fellow, who was my father's cow-boy. "Feel Willie" he was called, "feel" being Scotch for fool. It was the practice to give the servants a dose of medicine once a week. Feel Willie never could be induced to touch it. "I kenned a man once," Willie used to tell us, "that took a blue pill every night of his life, and a black draught in the morning, but"—and how Willie's face used to brighten up, as he added— "he dee'd (died) for a' that.[244]*

---

[243] "A grain of calomel or blue pill has been taken every night for more than forty years without other than good effects apparently, for one cannot argue much from fatty degeneration at the age of seventy-four (Med. Times ii., 1867). P 643 Phillips, C. D. F. 1830-1904. (1882). *Materia medica & therapeutics: inorganic substances.* London: J.& A. Churchill.

[244] *The Odd fellow's companion: devoted to the interests of the Independent Order of Odd Fellows.* (1876-1877) Columbus, Ohio: M.C. Lilley & Co. vol 18-19, pp264-267

Like any joke, the humor of Willies' lay in the exposure of a previously unacknowledged absurdity. Like the boy who could see that the emperor wasn't wearing any clothes, Willie was "feel" enough to see and point out the obvious, that taking mercury every day for forty years might kill you. Don't miss the fact that those ranch hands were given a weekly mercurial on a purely prophylactic basis, unconnected to any actual illness. Feel Willie's joke is proof, not of the deadliness of prolonged low level mercury exposure, a fact which is now generally accepted, but proof of the widespread habit of self-medication with blue pill and grey powder as "over the counter" medications which did not require a prescription and which were considered to be on a par with other home remedies.

The following excerpt in John Flint South's 1859 book, *Household surgery; or, hints on emergencies*[245] was typical of home health care books of the time in advising a home stock of mercurial medications. Of all of the possible examples of this sort, I have selected this one as we have evidence that Lewis Carroll ordered an earlier edition of this book for his home library.[246] Notice that the book advises that every family keep nitrate of mercury on hand for use as an ointment, and calomel for use as a wash, and that both calomel and mercurial or blue pill are included in the list of internal medicines which no family should ever be without.

---

[245] J. Flint (1859), *Household surgery; or, hints on emergencies.* 4th ed. London: John Murray, pp 2, 5

[246] Mar 4, 1856, *"Ordered Hints for Emergencies."*; Wakeling, E. (2001) *Lewis Carroll's Diaries, The Private Journals of Charles Lutwidge Dodgson*, Vol. 2, p 47

(2)

THE DOCTOR'S SHOP.

THE articles which all families, in the country, ought to be constantly provided with, are :—

Linseed meal⎫
Poppy heads⎬ For Poultices and Fomentations.
Camomile flowers⎭

Sticking or Adhesive Plaster or Strapping (all names of one and the same thing) for bringing together and binding up wounds.

Blister or Spanish Fly Plaster.

Wax and Oil (soothing)⎫
Spermaceti (same)⎪
Turner's or Calamine (absorbent)⎪
Oxide of Zinc (same)⎪ Cerate or
Yellow Basilicon or Resin (stimulating)⎬ Ointment.
Citron or Nitrate of Mercury (same)⎪
Lead (astringent)⎪
Gall (same)⎭

Sulphur

Opodeldoc or Soap⎫
Camphor⎬ Liniments
Mustard⎭

Sugar or Acetate of Lead⎫
Oxide of Zinc⎪
Calomel⎪
Sulphate of Zinc⎪
Sulphate of Copper⎬ For Washes.
Nitric Acid⎪
Solution of Chlorinated Soda⎪
———————————— Lime⎭

Two pair of tooth forceps, one for children, the
　other for adults, and
——— key instruments fitted for the like purpose.

Thus far for the Surgical Department of the
Doctor's Shop for home or foreign service.

But there are a few simple Family Medicines
with which no house should ever be unprovided :
such are :——

A Bottle of Castor Oil.
Lenitive Electuary, or Confection of Senna.
Calomel.
Tartarized Antimony.
Iodide of Potash.
Sulphate of Quinine.
Ipecacuanha Wine.
Mercurial or Blue Pill.
Rufous or Aloes and Myrrh Pills.
Powdered Rhubarb.
——————— Opium.
——————— Gum.
Oil of Cloves.
——— Peppermint.
Carbonate of Lime.
Croton Oil.
A pair of grain Scales, with weights from half a
　grain to two drachms.
A glass drop-measure and a glass two-ounce mea-
　sure.
A Dutch Tile, and a Spatula.

It is best to have all the fluids and powders in
stoppled bottles.

Such, then, are the furniture of the Doctor's

The renowned physician Dyce Duckworth summarized the rise and fall and resurrection of mercury in the years 1837 through 1897 in a paper focusing on the advances made by the sixtieth year of Queen Victoria's reign. It is a valuable perspective for our purposes as Queen Victoria's reign very nearly spans Lewis Carroll's lifetime. Carroll was only 5 years old when Queen Victoria took the throne in 1837, and he would die before her reign was over. Duckworth wrote that within the sixty years of 1837 through 1897,

The new school ventured to discard the hitherto vaunted virtues of this drug, pushed, as it was wont to be, often to salivation, and the induction thereby of a toxic cachexia. This again proved equally shocking to those who had learned to believe in the specific power of mercury as an agent cutting short and subduing inflammatory processes; but the new views prevailed, and materially altered the common practice of the day. Thus blood-letting and mercury were set aside, and without doubt, the results were in the main beneficient. But here, again, as often happens when great revolutions occur, extreme views do not contain the whole truth, and the pendulum swung so far that the idea grew in the minds of the profession that mercury was always a mischievous agent, and could be dispensed with under all conditions of disease. . . . From the standpoint of to-day we find that there still remains a place for the employment of mercury in many morbid conditions, and have learned that it can probably never be discarded from the list of efficient remedies in the hands of good clinical practitioners.[247]

Duckworth knew what he was talking about as he had been one of the men who had been responsible for giving the

---

[247] *The Practitioner, A Journal of Practical Medicine and Surgery,* old series Vol 58, new series Vol 5, Jaunary to June (1897) London: Cassell and Company, Limited, *The Advance in the Principles and Practice of Medicine during the Sixty Years of the Reign of Queen Victoria,* by Sir Dyce Duckworth, M.D. pp 593-611, p 597

pendulum a good hearty shove back to the status quo with his 1876 article in *The Practitioner*, *On the Modern Neglect of Calomel in Certain Disorders*, in which he had stated, "It cannot, I think, be doubted that calomel, either alone or in combination with jalap, colocynth, or scammony, constitutes one of the most certain and efficacious purgatives, clearing the entire portal system, producing a large flow of bile in the motions (though not manifestly acting as a strict cholagogue from the liver), and affording a measure of relief to the body unattainable by any other means."[248]

The problem, of course, was that just like Duckworth, those physicians who were convinced as to the efficacy of mercury were quite easily able to justify its continued use by slightly redefining its effect on the liver. It wasn't long before mercury was being touted as an "indirect" cholagogue, a substance which *indirectly* stimulated bile by clearing out the intestinal contents.[249] And of course, mercury continued to be used as a specific medication where the issue of bile was not involved. Mercury was used as a "specific" in every illness which Lewis Carroll would experience in his later years.

Lewis Carroll was an exceptionally healthy man in his early adult life, prompting a friend of his to write, "He had very good health and was seldom out of sorts for a day."[250] It may not have been merely good fortune, as Carroll was , during this time, a devotee of homeopathic medicine, and he would have seemed much healthier than the majority of his colleagues as he escaped the deleterious effects of the mercurial medications so many of

---

[248] *The Practitioner* Vol 17 (1876) London: Macmillan and Co., p 4
[249] Hale-White, W. (1892). *Materia medica, pharmacy, pharmacology and therapeutics.* Philadelphia: P. Blakiston, son & co.., pp 179-181; *The Practitioner.* (1905 v 75) London: John Brigg [etc.]., p128
[250] Elton, O. (1906). *Frederick York Powell: a life and a selection from his letters and occasional writings.* Oxford: The Clarendon press., p 365

his colleagues would have been exposed to. Despite his good health, there *were* issues suggesting the possibility of an underlying nervous derangement. He had a "hesitation of speech", and had suffered from partial deafness since his episodes of brain fever as an infant and mumps as a child, and he had had problems with his right eye as far back as 1856. He also had an extremely poor memory for faces, which if you will recall, is a common condition in autism spectrum disorders. Problems with facial recognitions are not limited to those with autism, but may also occur in *mental* disorders such as obsessive compulsive disorder, bipolar disorder and schizophrenia, as well as in *physical* disorders, such as head injury, penetrating brain injury and dementia. There are specific areas in our brains which help us to recognize a face, and damage to these areas can impair facial recognition.[251] Carroll was aware of his problem, writing in his diary in 1881 that a woman he knew had to introduce herself to him when they met on the beach, "as I have no memory for faces."[252] His nephew told similar stories,

people used to say (most unjustly) that he was intentionally short-sighted. One night he went up to London to dine with a friend, whom he had only recently met. The next morning a gentleman greeted him as he was walking. "I beg your pardon," said Mr. Dodgson, "but you have the advantage of me. I have no remembrance of having ever seen you before this moment." "That is very strange," the other replied, "for I was your host last night!" Such little incidents as this happened more than once.[253]

---

[251] Transcranial direct current stimulation of the dorsolateral **prefrontal** cortex modulates repetition suppression to unfamiliar faces: an ERP study, Lafontaine MP, Théoret H, Gosselin F, Lippé S, PLoS One. 2013 Dec 4;8(12):e81721; Face memory impairments in patients with frontal lobe damage, Rapcsak SZ, Nielsen L, Littrell LD, Glisky EL, Kasniak AW, Laguna JF, Neurology 2001 Oct 9;57(7):1168-75.
[252] Wakeling, E. (2001) Lewis Carroll's Diaries, The Private Journals of Charles Lutwidge Dodgson Vol 7, p 365.

Years before, when Carroll was still a young professor, a student of his had presented him with a copy of Thomas Hood's *Poems of Wit and Humor* as a gift. After a poem about a profoundly deaf woman, Hood quoted the following passage, addressed specifically to those readers afflicted with deafness, "In lew whereof the Deaf Man, as testified by mine own Experience, is regaled with an inward Musick that is not vouchsafed unto a Person who hath the complete Usage of his Ears."[254] Hood discussed the passage as if it referred to ringing in the ears, but it's author may have meant actual music, as modern day neurologists know that complex auditory hallucinations of music, tunes and melodies often fill the void left by dysfunctions in hearing, just as complex visual hallucinations often fill the void left by blind spots in vision.[255] The generation by the brain of complex visual hallucinations in the absence of visual input is known as Charles Bonnet Syndrome, a phenomenon which is widely under reported because of the subjects' fears of being thought mentally deranged—as you can imagine. But those who suffer from Charles Bonnet Syndrome are often psychologically normal, with full insight into the unreal nature of their hallucinations. These hallucinations can appear in a spectrum from simple lights, colors, lines and shapes, such as the moving geometric patterns commonly seen in migraine, to the more complex, such as musical notes, letters or flowers overlying walls or other surrounding

[253] Collingwood, S. Dodgson. (1899). *The life and letters of Lewis Carroll (Rev. C.L. Dodgson)*. New York: The Century Co., p 267.

[254] Hood, T. (1847). *Poems of wit and humour.* London: E. Moxon.

[255] Bergman J, Pashinian A, Weizman A, Poyurovsky M ,*The beneficial effect of escitalopram on obsessive-compulsive-related musical hallucinations in elderly patients with hearing impairment: a case series*, Int Clin Psychopharmacol., 2014 May 7. [Epub ahead of print]; Reichert DP, Series P, Storkey AJ, Charles Bonnet syndrome: evidence for a generative model in the cortex? PLOS Comput Biol., 2013;9(7)

objects, to the complex visual hallucination of walking, talking people, strangely, often in miniature. "Lilliputian hallucinations" are a hallmark of the syndrome.[256] Interestingly, Lewis Carroll would write of experiencing these forms of hallucination as a character within his own stories, seeing letters on leaves, seeing fairies, and hearing the music of the flowers when he was in an "eerie" state of mind. It makes you wonder if there isn't also a spectrum of imagination, a gradation, which begins with imagination and little by little, nearly imperceptibly, passes into an unusually vivid and compelling imagination, before it becomes an intrusive day dreaming, and then, hallucination.

In the summer of 1874, just when mercury was making a strong resurgence, Carroll began to complain of more serious issues, such as "neuralgia".[257] From 1874 to 1876, in the same time period in which Carroll began to work trying to restore his ruined photographic negatives, Carroll wrote *the Hunting of the Snark*, a poem which was considered to be "readable, though not generally intelligible,"[258] a fact which may be accounted for by its unusual means of composition, described by Lewis Carroll as follows,

> *I was walking on a hill-side, alone, one bright summer day, when suddenly there came into my head one line of verse—one solitary line—'For the Snark was a Boojum, you see.' I knew not what it meant, then" I know not what it means, now: but I wrote it down: and, some time afterwards, the rest of the stanza occurred to me, that being its last line: and so by degrees, at odd*

---

[256] Schneider MA, Scheidner MD, Strange sightings: is it Charles Bonnet syndrome? Nursing, 2013 Jul;43(7):52-5; Sacks, O. W. (2012). *Hallucinations*. New York and Toronto: Alfred A. Knopf.

[257] Wakeling, E. (2001) *Lewis Carroll's Diaries, The Private Journals of Charles Lutwidge Dodgson*, Vol. 6, April 1868-1876, p. 340.

[258] *The London Quarterly Review*, Vol XLVII October 1876, and January 1877, London: Printed for the Proprietors, p247

moments during the next year or two, the rest of the poem pieced itself together, that being its last stanza. And since then, periodically, I have received courteous letters from strangers, begging to know whether 'the Hunting of the Snark' is an allegory, or contains some hidden moral, or is a political satire: and for all such questions I have but one answer, "I don't know!" [259]

It is not surprising that strangers were trying to puzzle out the meaning of the *Hunting of the Snark*, following so closely, as it did, on the heels of his incredibly meaning dense satires published in 1874, *The evaluation of* π, *The Dynamics of a Parti-cle*, *Facts, Figures and Fancies*, *The New Belfry*, *The Vision of the Three T's*, and *The Blank Cheque*. Carroll had written then, "everything has a moral, if you chose to look for it," and he had listed those writers whose work contained a moral by percentage, "In Wordsworth, a good half of every poem is devoted to the Moral: in Byron, a smaller proportion: in Tupper," who Carroll acknowledged as a genius worthy of tribute, "the whole."[260] The question in Carroll's case is what percentage of his work is the moral, and what percentage is that strange inner voice that spoke to him without imparting any understanding of meaning?

I have a good friend who began to experience the auditory hallucination of a man's voice after a brain surgery and infection resulted in an epileptic seizure disorder. The first time she heard the voice, she thought someone might be in the house with her, but she soon came to realize, as do the sufferers of Charles Bonnet Syndrome, that the voice was not real. It is a distinctive voice, and one which she recognizes when she hears it. She says

[259] Scott, C. *The Theatre: a monthly review and magazine.* New Series Vol IX January to June 1887, London: Carson & Comerford, *"Alice" on the Stage* by Lewis Carroll, pp 179-184, p 181
[260] Carroll, L. (1874). *Notes by an Oxford chiel.* Oxford:: James Parker and Co., p 22.

that the voice is "Difficult to retain and disappears like a dream, but an essence is left over. It's very dream like. The words don't make sense in the context of reality but the sentences are basic sentences." They are, she says, very much like those Carroll reported as dream suggestions, such as his "and the Snark was a Boojum you see," and "it ran in families, just like the love of pastry." There is no evidence that Carroll heard the phrases he composed into *the Hunting of the Snark* in any voice but his own inner voice, but there *is* evidence that he considered the generation of these nonsense phrases as coming from an internal, yet alien source, a subject which we will examine in more depth in the next chapter.

In May of 1885, Carroll wrote in his diary "In the morning I experienced, for the second time, that odd optical affection of seeing moving fortifications, followed by a headache."[261] June 1888 "This morning, on getting up, I experienced that curious optical effect, of "seeing fortifications," discussed in Dr. Latham's book on "bilious headache."[262] In this instance, it affected the right eye only, at the outer corner; and there was no headache." In December of 1888 he wrote that he had experienced optical fortifications with a blind spot. In September of 1889, he saw the "fortifications" again, "but no headache followed."[263] In Sept 1891, he wrote, "Last evening I had another experience of "seeing fortifications."[264] In a seeming progression, at the end of the

---

[261] Wakeling, E. (2001) *Lewis Carroll's Diaries, The Private Journals of Charles Lutwidge Dodgson*, Vol 8, p 201

[262] Latham, P. W. (1873) *On Nervous of Sick-Headache Its Varieties and Treatment*, Cambridge: Brighton Bell and Co.; On Sick-Headache, Latham PW, Br Med J. 1873 Jan 4;1(627):7-8; The Pathology of **Sick-Headache**, **Latham** PW, Br Med J. 1873 Feb 1;1(631):113-4.

[263] Wakeling, E. (2001) *Lewis Carroll's Diaries, The Private Journals of Charles Lutwidge Dodgson*, Vol 8 p 483

[264] Wakeling, E. (2001) *Lewis Carroll's Diaries, The Private Journals of Charles Lutwidge Dodgson*, Vol 8 p 580

year, New Years' Eve, or New Years' Day, he had an "epileptiform" attack "which left me with a sort of headache, and not feeling my usual self, for a week or ten days." When he had a second such attack, also in winter, his doctor ascribed them as possibly due to the coldness of the day, and advised him not to travel at Christmas.[265]

As you may have noticed in Lewis Carroll's diary, migraine was originally called a bilious headache. This is because it was believed that bilious headaches were the result of a sluggish digestive system, and that the best treatment would be that which promoted good digestion. In the 1840s and 1850s, the theories on the cause of bilious headache vacillated between that of a reflex neuralgia in the alimentary canal causing a disturbance of the fifth-nerve of the brain, and that of a build-up of biliary poisons in circulation causing an irritation of the brain. Either way, mercury was the go-to drug to solve the problem. Before Lewis Carroll was born, sick headache had been treated with large doses of strong mercurials like calomel, and while, by the 1870s and 1880s aggressive treatment with calomel was less common, it remained a common practice to take a small dose of calomel or blue pill to prevent or to mitigate an attack of sick headache.[266] The theory of causation was changing from a purely hepatic theory and the name bilious headache would be used less and less until it would be mostly forgotten, but as this excerpt on Migraine in the 1914 *Treatise on Clinical Medicine*, shows,

---

[265] Wakeling, E. (2001) *Lewis Carroll's Diaries, The Private Journals of Charles Lutwidge Dodgson* Vol 8, pp 255, 549-553, 600
[266] Mease J. (1832) *On the causes, cure, and prevention of sick headache.* 5th ed Philadelphia: H. H. Porter, pp 9-11; Drewry G. (1875) *Common-sense Management of the Stomach.* London: Henry S. King, pp 122-123; Ringer, S. (1878) A handbook of Therapeutics. London H. K. Lewis, p 243; Hamilton, A. McLane. (1888). *The modern treatment of headaches.* Detroit, Mich.: G. S. Davis., p 15;

mercury as a treatment of migraine headache had incredible staying power,

All severe cases, without exception, are chronic dyspeptics, and of this one of the commonest symptoms is chronic constipation. A mercurial laxative, such as a 5-gr. blue pill at night, with a saline in the morning to secure its action is a weekly prescription of mine which I strongly insist upon in every case, to be kept up for months. I am sure that we do not possess a more certain intestinal antiseptic than a mercurial cathartic, and I never feel satisfied when a patient for any reasons declines to persevere in its employment.[267]

The cause of migraine is unknown, but the fact that migraine is accompanied by bioelectrical abnormalities in the brain has caused some researchers to hypothesize a connection between migraine and epilepsy.[268]   An epileptic seizure is a massive electrical discharge originating from within the brain. Modern day neurologists have conducted animal experiments proving that exposure to mercury in utero increases the tendency to epileptic seizure in parallel to the mercury concentrations in cortical tissues, and people or animals with acute or chronic mercury poisoning often experience epileptiform seizures.[269]   This is because our brains are chemical/electrical systems, and not only

---

[267] Thomson, W.H. (1914) *A Treatise on Clinical Medicine*, Philadelphia and London: W. B. Saunders Company, pp 549-550

[268] *Prophylactic treatment in children with migraine presenting changes in electrophysiological and cerebral blood flow examinations: preliminary report*, Biernawska J, Miller K, Pierzchata K, Neurol Neurochip Pol. 1999;33 Suppl 5:67-76

[269] *Effects of continuous low-dose exposure to organic and inorganic mercury during development on epileptogenicity in rats*, Szász A, Barna B, Gajda Z,, De Visscher G, Galbács Z, Kirsh-Volders M, Szente M, *Neuortoxicology*, 2002 Jul;23(2): 197-206; *Methylmercury: a potential environmental risk factor contributing to epileptogenesis*, Yuan Y, *Neurotoxicology*, 2012 Jan;33(1): 119-126

does mercury effect the transmission of chemical messages, it can enhance the amplitude and frequency of the brains' synaptic currents.[270] This does not prove that *Lewis Carroll's* epileptiform seizures were caused by mercury, but it cannot be ignored that the treatments for migraine in the 1800s were likely to bring on epileptic seizures. And then there was that troubling persistence of epileptic insanity, a psychical degeneration of epileptics, which ranged from a stupor in the days following a seizure, to "a dreamy confused state of mind not unlike that of a somnambulist", an abnormal state of mind in which the afflicted might seem, to all appearances rational, acting and speaking accordingly, while all the while feeling themselves as in a dream.[271] This state could last from hours to months.

---

[270] *Mercury-induced toxicity of rat cortical neurons is mediated through N-Methyl-D-Aspartate receptors*, Xu F, Farkas S, Kortbeek S, Zhang FX, Chen L, Zamponi GW, Syed NI, *Mol Brain* 2012 Sep 14;5:30
[271] *The London Medical Record*, Nov. 16, 1885, Article 4797, *Hönigsberger on the responsibility of epileptics*, pp 463-464

Sylvie and Bruno

The number of lunatic books is as finite as the number of lunatics.

-Lewis Carroll, Sylvie and Bruno Concluded

Carroll's next and last major works of fiction, the fairy stories, *Sylvie and Bruno* (1889) and *Sylvie and Bruno Concluded* (1893), incorporated his recurring themes of theory of mind and transcendence of time and space. Just as *Alice's Adventures in Wonderland* had its beginning as a shorter, simpler fairy tale, *Sylvie and Bruno* had a first iteration, a charming but insignificant fairy story called *Bruno's Revenge* which Carroll wrote in 1867 for Aunt Judy's Magazine.[272] In the story Bruno was a fairy boy who planted a beautiful garden at the river's edge for his fairy sister, Sylvie, "revenge" being a baby language corruption of the words "river's edge." Lewis Carroll appeared as himself, and both observed and interacted with the fairies.

In either 1873 or 1874, Carroll would write later, he decided to build on *Bruno's Revenge* to make it a longer and more important work. *Alice* had been celebrated as a breath of fresh air because it was *apparently* without lesson or moral. This time around Lewis Carroll took pains to be less obscure. He told his readers not to regard the work wholly as a book of thoughtless nonsense, but to look for hidden meanings. There could be no doubt about the weighty metaphysical nature of subjects added to the story in any case, as Carroll helpfully indexed the subjects addressed at the end of the book, detailing both the medicine and the jam, so to

---

[272] Gatty, A. *Aunt Judy's May-Day Volume.* (1868) London: Bell and Daldy Bruno's Revenge by Lewis Carroll, pp 65-78

speak, so that the index listed such technical subjects such as the inverted position of the brain, inversion of images by the eyes, reversal of time, free will, nerve force and conceivably non-existent relative weight alongside the more nonsensical children's subjects such as boots for horizontal weather, the logic of crocodiles, and how to amuse young frogs.

Likewise, if there had been any doubt that strange events were especially likely to be apprehended by Carroll's characters in the twilight state of mind which accompanies the act, not of being asleep, but of falling asleep, Carroll spelled it out in the preface to *Sylvie and Bruno Concluded*. The story assumed three states of human consciousness, Carroll explained, the ordinary state (in which one did *not* see fairies), an "eerie" state in which one *did* see fairies, and a trance like state in which a person could travel into the fairy world, ("by actual transference of their immaterial essence, such as we meet with in 'Esoteric Buddhism'"). To further complicate matters, the story also assumed different states of *fairy* consciousness, the ordinary state (in which one did *not* see human beings), and an "eerie" state in which fairies could see either the actual human being, or their immaterial essence, depending on which world they were in, the actual world, or Fairyland. The whole of Sylvie and Bruno is a complicated meditation on "eerie" dream-like states, as can be seen by the following table composed by Carroll himself:

Vol. I.	Historian's Locality and State.			Other characters.
pp. 1— 16	In train		c	Chancellor (c) p. 2.
33— 55	do.		c	
65— 79	do.		c	
83— 99	At lodgings		c	
105—117	On beach		c	
119—183	At lodgings		c	S. and B. (b) pp. 158—163. Professor (b) p. 169.
190—221	In wood		b	Bruno (b) pp. 198—220.
225—233	do. sleep-walking · .		c	S. and B. (b).
247—253	Among ruins		c	do. (b).
262, 263	do. dreaming . .	a		
263—269	do. sleep-walking		c	S. B. and Professor in Human form.
270 . . .	In street		b	
279—294	At station, &c.		b	S. and B. (b).
304—323	In garden		c	S. B. and Professor (b).
329—344	On road, &c.	a		S. and B. in Human form.
345—356	In street, &c.	a		
361—382	In wood		b	S. and B. (b).
Vol. II.				
pp. 4— 18	In garden		b	S. and B. (b).
47— 52	On road		b	do. (b).
53— 78	do.		b	do. in Human form.
79 — 92	do.		b	do. (b).
152—211	In drawing-room	a		do. in Human form.
212—246	do.		c	do. (b).
262—270	In smoking-room		c	do. (b).
304—309	In wood		b	do. (a) ; Lady Muriel (b).
311—345	At lodgings		c	
351—399	do.		c	
407—end.	do.		b	

(a-ordinary state, b-eerie state, c-trance/transference)

Carroll, interested as he was in medical research, and having suffered his own epileptiform seizures and minor optical hallucinations, could not have been unaware that the term "dreamy state" was used by neurologists in the 1880's to describe the "intellectual aura" that presaged some epileptic seizures, a state of "over-consciousness" which was characterized by hallucinations more complex than the more usual phantom smells, hearing of voices, or seeing of faces.[273] It was a "peculiar

---

[273] Ophthalmological Society of the United Kingdom. *Transactions of the Ophthalmological Society of the United Kingdom.* Vol 6 (1886) London: J. & A. Churchill, *Diseases of the Nervous System, Being the Bowman Lecture,* by Dr. J. Hughlings Jackson, pp 1-22

hazy condition marked by dreamy romantic ideas", and the people who experienced it walked through life for hours, even for months, at a time, like sleep-walkers, mentally deranged, but to all appearances, rational.[274]

It was an interesting choice of subject matter for Carroll to make, but then again, Carroll had been interested in the overlaps between consciousness, dreaming, and insanity since his University days. Recall his earlier 1856 diary entry,

> the Feb 9. (Sat). Query: when we are dreaming and, as often happens, have a dim consciousness of the fact and try to wake, do we not say and do things which in waking life would be insane? May we not then sometimes define insanity as an inability to distinguish which is the waking and which the sleeping life? We often dream without the least suspicion of unreality: "Sleep hath its own world", and it is often as lifelike as the other.

For years—ever since he had revealed the strange nature of his composition of the *Hunting of the Snark* in an 1887 *Theatre* article—Lewis Carroll had been insisting that he had not actually sat down and intentionally created any of his fiction, that it had all occurred to him as he was falling asleep, or upon waking, or that his ideas had come to him out of the blue while he was walking or otherwise occupied. He wrote about *Alice's Adventures in Wonderland*, for example, that, "In writing it out, I added many fresh ideas, which seemed to grow of themselves upon the original stock; and many more added themselves when, years afterwards, I wrote it all over again for publication; but (this may

---

[274] Hart, E. Abraham. *London medical record.* London. Vol 13 (1865), Articl 4797, Honigsberger on the Responsibility of Epileptics, by E. F. Willoughby, pp 463-465.

interest some readers of "Alice" to know; every such idea and nearly every word of the dialogue *came of itself*.

Sometimes an idea comes at night when I have had to get up and strike a light to note it down—sometimes when out on a lonely winter walk, when I have had to stop, and with half-frozen fingers jot down a few words which should keep the new-born idea from perishing—but whenever or however it comes, it *comes of itself*. I cannot set invention going like a clock, by any voluntary winding up; nor do I believe that any *original* writing (and what other writing is worth preserving?) was ever so produced."[275]

Carroll demonstrated this act of somnambulant creation as his doppelganger Professor character in Sylvie and Bruno, who composed the following nonsense rhyme while falling asleep on a train. "I thought I saw—" I murmered sleepily: and then the phase insisted on conjugating itself, and ran into "you thought you saw—he thought he saw—" and then it suddenly went off into a song:--

> *"He thought he saw an Elephant,*
> *That practised on a fife;*
> *He looked again, and found it was*
> *A letter from his wife,*
> *'At length I realize,' he said,*
> *'The bitterness of Life!'"*

This poem composed on the verge of sleep is a pretty good allegory for the *Sylvie and Bruno* novels in whole, surreal nonsense, incomprehensible plotting, and a bitter aftertaste. The public had expected to welcome the book and instead turned away in confused disappointment. It wasn't merely that the book

---

[275] Scott, C. *The Theatre: a monthly review and magazine.* New Series Vol IX January to June 1887, London: Carson & Comerford, *"Alice" on the Stage* by Lewis Carroll, pp 179-184

contained grave realities more appropriate for a sermon ("the author has avowed his belief that from the merry side of life young folks should be led to look upon the graver realities which are part of the lot of all humanity"), it was that the book was such an odd mixture of childish nonsense and unpleasant adult truths, such as illness and death, both repulsive in parts and incomprehensible in whole.[276]

The reviews were almost overwhelmingly negative, and the reviewers struggled to explain their shock and dismay,

But something has gone wrong with one of our own humorists. Can you fancy the Walrus and the Carpenter discussing the morality of play-going, and deciding that the fear of sudden death in a theatre ought to convince the timid that it is wrong for them to go there? Surely, Mr. Carroll, that is the last idea in the world to put into the head of a child, especially at pantomime time; but perhaps nobody expects children to read the preface of Sylvie and Bruno. –The New Review.[277]

Sylvie and Bruno" is a complicated excursion in mental philosophy, in which we are allegorically "taught" all sorts of things, and in which the topsy-turveydom of fairyland marches along, not incongruously,--for that is allowable and enjoyable,-- but foolishly, with realities of no interest whatever. The preface sets the self-respecting reader against the book from the outset; in it we are told not to regard the book wholly as a book of thoughtless nonsense, but to look out for hidden meanings; but when the time comes, there is no meaning discernable, unless by harder work than any author has a right to demand of his followers, while the nonsense seems pumped up and is not the hearty spontaneous article. –The American[278]

---

[276] *The Critic: an illustrated monthly review of literature, art, and life.* New York: The Critic Company . v.13 new series 1890 Jan-jun, p 152
[277] *The New review.* Vol 2 (Jan-June 1890), London: Longmans, Green and Co., pp 188-189
[278] Barker, W., Thompson, R. Ellis. (1881-1900). *The American: a national*

The positive reviews were short and attempted to claim "inconsistency of plot" as positive evidence of nonsense. Carroll admitted that he had stitched together odds and ends of a chaos of notes that he had made over the years, including random events and conversations that he had transcribed from memory, such as the measurement of a dead mouse, phrases which had occurred to him in a dream (such as the innocuous "it often runs in families, just as a love of pastry does"), and full transcripts of conversations overheard between such varied groups as little boys and little girls, university undergraduates, and a poet laureate. He admitted to a speech copied verbatim from the columns of "the Standard" as made by Sir William Harcourt, and much more. It was, as Carroll wrote, a "tale of bricks." There was a saying that was popular in Carroll's time, that "stones and bricks are valuable things, very valuable; but they are not beautiful or useful till the hand of the architect has given them a form, and the cement of the bricklayer has knit them together." [279] All of Carroll's notes and dream suggestions, and fragments of conversations were the bricks, and he had tried to cement them together as he always had, but it wasn't working for him as well as it had before.

The Philosopher John Locke said that it was just this sort of disorderly jumbling together of unconnected ideas, that characterized madness, but *was* Carroll mad? Perhaps it was all an intentional experiment that failed. It is clear that he studied theories of mind, and used that knowledge to purposely and deliberately cultivate madness in his early writings, with fantastic success. But what of his later writings? Did he fail to see the

---

journal. Vol 19 (1889-1990) Philadelphia: The American company, limited, p 317

[279] Martin, A., Lewis, S. (1839). *Woman's mission.* 4th ed. London: John W. Parker, p 62.

inconsistencies of his story or is the fault our own, that we have failed to follow him? The *Sylvie and Bruno* books are far too convoluted to answer that question "unless by harder work than any author has a right to demand." To paraphrase Carroll's characters *in Sylvie and Bruno*, we generally admire most the teachers we don't quite understand.[280] That of course, is because we think that our failure to understand is due to our own limitations, and that the material and therefore the teacher is above us, and *not* that the material is flawed. If it is true that Carroll had all along taken his inspiration from subconscious sources, as he has claimed, and linked these "pieces" together just as they happened to fall, his previous genius, his *romancement*, in knitting them together was beginning to fail— the *Sylvie and Bruno* books were repeatedly described as disjointed and lacking in unity.

Without getting too tangled up in the knot-like puzzles of the *Sylvie and Bruno* plot, the most interesting part of the book for our purposes is what it can tell us about Carroll's appreciation of his own mental state, because *Sylvie and Bruno* started out as a story in which Carroll was self-identified as the narrator. In the original story, *Bruno's Revenge*, when Bruno asked the narrator his name, he responded, "My name is Lewis Carroll." *Bruno's Revenge* was included nearly as written in the body of *Sylvie and Bruno* (as chapter 14, *Fairy Sylvie* and chapter 15, *Bruno's Revenge*) with only a few changes, one of which was the obfuscation of Lewis Carroll's self-identification. That passage was changed from "My name is Lewis Carroll" to, "I told him my name."[281] In *Sylvie and Bruno*, not only has Carroll obscured his identity and added the three states of human consciousness

---

[280] Carroll, L. (1889). *Sylvie and Bruno*. London: Macmillan, p 182
[281] Ibid., p 198.

(ordinary, eerie and trance-like), instead of one Professor character, there are now *three*, the Professor, the Old/Other Professor, and Mein Herr (a retired Professor). What Furniss, at the least, has made clear in his illustrations is that each character is an older version of the one before. Carroll keeps dropping hints that this is so, as well, in passages like this one, in which the narrator is describing Mein Herr showing Lady Muriel how to make an inside-out Fortunatus' purse (so that all of the wealth of the outside world would be inside of it):

Mein Herr making a handkerchief Fortunatus' purse for Lady Muriel
"Something wonderful like Fortunatus' purse? That will give you—when it is made—wealth beyond your wildest dreams; but it will not give you Time!"

Describing Lady Muriel and Mein Herr, the narrator writes,

She looked so strangely like a child, puzzling over a difficult lesson, and Mein Herr had become, for the moment, so strangely like the old Professor, that I felt utterly bewildered: the 'eerie' feeling was on me it its full force and I felt almost impelled to say "Do you understand it Sylvie?" However I checked myself by a great effort, and let the dream (if indeed it was a dream) go on to its end."[282]

Because the narrator is experiencing an abnormal mental state, he momentarily experienced himself and Lady Muriel in an earlier state, when he was the Old Professor, and she, the fairy child Sylvie.   As the story makes clear, the narrator is the Professor, although it is not clear which one, an intentional literary device obscuring the fact that he is *all three* Professor characters, each one further along "in the eternal cycle of change."   And not only is each one further along in a progression of change, each one is further along in a progression through the three abnormal mental states and towards madness.   The younger professor is very "dreamy", the other/old Professor has continual "eerie feelings" and has moments of concern that he must guard against being considered a lunatic, and the retired Professor, Mein Herr, is a confirmed lunatic.   The increasingly intensified versions of the Professor, culminating in a Germanic lunacy is evocative of Carroll's earlier *Photography Extraordinaire*.

As if the three states of consciousness and the intersection of the narrator with the three variants of the Professor were not enough complication for the story, the fragment of song which comes into the mind of the narrator/professor character as he

---

[282] Carroll, L. (1893). *Sylvie and Bruno concluded.* London: Macmillan and Co, p 103

falls asleep is attributed to yet another character who appears later in the book, that of the Mad Gardener, the songs of which were considered to be "the best of the good things" in a book which was otherwise, unquestionably a failure. The songs of the mad gardener scattered throughout the book were deemed "almost worthy to stand by the side of the song the White Knight sang to Alice in the realms of the Looking Glass . . . a dexterous mixture of irrelevance of thought and conventionality."[283] Why a gardener? Consider again Lewis Carroll's walk through Bruno's garden, a garden in which the holes left by insects form letters in the leaves, and in which the flowers spell out sentences, *if* you are in an eerie state.[284] And, if you had any remaining doubt about the genesis of Carroll's mad hatter, Carroll's mad gardener should answer it finally, for the gardener is Lewis Carroll's personification of that little voice which composes his most surreal nonsense as he is falling asleep, a conduit to and from an internal madness. The only difference in the function of the characters is that the mad gardener composes *from* the dream world, and the mad hatter lives entirely *within* Lewis Carroll's mad dream.

One last thing to take note of before we move on, the Professor characters, In stark contrast to the beautifully drawn figures of the other characters, all have big round heads with round staring eyes, something which doesn't make sense until you consider how moon-like they are. And it wasn't an accident. "Your face is large and round like the moon" Bruno tells Carroll, "I see a little twinkle in one of your eyes—just like the moon."[285] Just like the moon, the lunatic's guardian satellite, and changing as he goes on.

---

[283] The Spectator Vol 64 (1890) London: John Campbell, p 93
[284] Gatty, A. *Aunt Judy's annual volume.* Vol 4-5 (1868) London: Bell and Daldy, pp. 65-78
[285] Ibid, p 72.

Sylvie and Bruno look on as the Other Professor tries to wake the Professor

Sylvie and Bruno (in human form) talk with Mein Herr

All of this literary analysis is of only passing interest. The greater issue is not the story of the story, but the story of the man, the significance of Carroll's own apprehension of his own increasing mental illness. And the more important question—*If* Carroll believed that he was developing a problem, what would he have done?

He almost certainly would have resorted to the blue pill.

Doctors of the time were nearly unanimous in their belief that a disordered state of the bodily functions, manifesting as headache, sleeplessness, and a change in manner or behavior, were the first symptoms of an impending mental disturbance, which, *if treated medically*, could forestall a more serious problem.[286] "Most persons," wrote William Benjamin Carpenter in his 1875 Principles of Mental Physiology, have experienced a depression which has been cleared up by a dose of blue pill, and have experienced the change as like "a cloud passing away (as it were) from the mental vision, a weight being lifted off 'the spirits.'"[287] The belief that a small dose of calomel, blue pill or grey powder could provide "sometimes very remarkable results" in the treatment of *adult* nervous irritability and depression, was so widespread that it was not infrequently used in the treatment of *children*. ("I have seen a quarter of a grain of calomel, with a seidlitz powder next morning, change as naughty a little girl as you wouldn't wish to see into a perfect little angel.") [288] Or consider this exchange from the autobiography of one man being treated by his doctor after a lapse in sanity due to a blow to the head, "Oh, then I must have been as mad as a March hare." "No

---

[286] *Familiar views of lunacy and lunatic life: with hints on the personal care and management of those who are afflicted with temporary or permanent derangement.* (1850) London: John W. Parker. pp 41-42

[287] Carpenter, W. Benjamin. (1875). *Principles of mental physiology: with their applications to the training and discipline of the mind, and the study of its morbid conditions.* 2d ed. London: H.S. King & Co.. p 659

[288] The Cavendish Lecture on Elimination & its Uses in Preventing and Curing Disease, T. Lauder Brunton, Br Med J. 1891 June 20; 1(1590): 1321–1326.

matter; you're improving now. Take a blue pill to-night as well as the bath. The effect is surprising…"[289] The theory of the cause of the bodily derangement had changed from that of the failure of the liver to properly secrete bile, to congestion of blood in the head, but the end result of mercurial treatment was the same. Other theories, such as uric acid in the blood, received the same treatment, "After a blue-pill at night and a seidlitz powder next morning, the outlook is rosier."[290] In fact, blue pill was so widely prescribed for every eventuality that when social reformers suggested disbanding private lunacy facilities with in-house physicians , the defenders of those institutions fought back by citing a one-size-fits-all over reliance on mercurial medications by the public institutions, complaining that "the consulting physician in three different cases—one of asthma, one of acute mania, and the third of injury to the knee-joint—ordered a blue pill and a black draught for each."[291]

At least in the case of the mania, the consulting physician would have been squarely in line with the long-term beliefs and practice of the Lunacy Commission. Anthony Ashley Cooper, the 7th Earl of Shaftesbury, who presided over the Lunacy Commission from the years 1828 to at least the year 1880 believed very strongly that "if people would only take a little more blue-pill, there would soon be an appreciable diminution in the gross amount of madness."[292] Lord Shaftesbury was such a beloved and

[289] (1895). *Jack Westropp: an autobiography*. London: Downey. Vol 1, p 55
[290] Fothergill, J. Milner. (1890). *The diseases of sedentary and advanced life: a work for medical and lay readers*. London: Baillière, Tindall, and Cox, p 189
[291] Br Med J. Jun 21, 1884; 1(1225): 1208–1210, Reports of Societies, Pp1209-1210
[292] Burdett, H. C. (1891). *Hospitals and asylums of the world: their origin, history, construction, administration, management, and legislation* Vol II, London: J. & A. Churchill, p 207; Bucknill, J. Charles. (1880). *The care of the insane and their legal control*. 2nd ed. London: Macmillan.

prominent member of British society that his 80th birthday, on the 28th of April 1881, was celebrated as a national event.[293] And as a beloved figure, Shaftesbury's belief in the usefulness of blue pill at the first signs of an emotional disorder was often echoed by the public, notably, by Henry Kingsley, the friend of Carroll's who suggested he publish *Alice*. Kingsley wrote in his 1859 novel *Geoffrey Hamlyn*, "That evening was the first thoroughly unhappy evening, I think, that Sam ever passed in his life. I am inclined to imagine that his digestion was out of order. If any of my readers ever find themselves in the same state of mind that he was in that night, let them be comforted by considering that there is always a remedy at hand, before which evil thoughts and evil tempers of all kinds fly like mist before the morning sun. How many serious family quarrels, marriages out of spite, alterations of wills, and secessions to the Church of Rome, might have been prevented by a gentle dose of blue pill!"[294]

Blue pill for lunacy was close to home for Carroll—It can't be overlooked that Lewis Carroll's favorite uncle, Skeffington Luttwidge, was a long-time member of the Lunacy Commission. He had, in fact, been the Secretary presiding over the much cited and comprehensive *Further Report of the Commissioners in Lunacy to the Lord Chancellor, presented to both Houses of Parliament in 1847.*[295] As a part of this 500 page report, the Commissioners had attempted to ascertain the medical treatment of the insane, and, unsurprisingly, mercury in some form was one

---

[293] Hodder, E. (1886). *The life and work of the seventh Earl of Shaftesbury, K.G.* London: Cassell & company, limited., vol 3, p 421

[294] Kingsley, H. (1859). *The recollections of Geoffry Hamlyn.* Cambridge: Macmillan, Vol 2, pp 231-232

[295] Great Britain. Lunacy Commission., . (1847). *Further report of the Commissioners in Lunacy, to the Lord Chancellor: presented to both houses of Parliament by command of her majesty.* London: Shaw and Sons, printers, Fetter Lane.

of the remedies most frequently mentioned in the treatment of insanity. The remedies were broken down into 4 areas of insanity related concern, the treatment of mania, melancholia, epilepsy and paralysis. I list mentions of the use of mercurial treatments here in excerpts which necessarily omit the mention of other remedies:

Remedies used in the Treatment of Mania: Dr. Sutherland of St. Luke's Hospital, "mercury is especially useful in all forms of the disease, for its purgative effects, for stimulating the liver, and for equalizing the circulation."—Mr. Casson of Hull and East Riding Retreat, "a dose of calomel" and "alterative doses of some mercurial, with a small quantity of opium, and sometimes pushed so far as to affect the gums slightly."—Sir Morison of Surrey County Asylum, recourse to laxative medicines including calomel—Mr. Watson of Cumberland County Asylum, "regulation of the diegestive organs, by the blue pill, rhubarb, aloes &c., together with the cold shower bath, appear to me to be the priniciples on which we ought to base our treatment and which I have found most successful."—Dr. Button of Dorest County Asylum, "purgatives, including calomel"—Dr. Tyerman of Cornwall County Asylum, calomel in the stage of high delirious excitement, and ung. Hydrarg. Deuto-iodureti to the forehead in the stage of incoherency and delusions—Dr. Bryan of Hoxton House, "purgatives have been found extremely useful, combined, when required, with blue pill, as an alterative. . . The blue pill, with the compound of colocynth, and all the milder aperients "are constantly administered with the best effect."—Mr. Smith of Hadham Palace Asylum, "purgatives of calomel and pulvis. Ipecac comp. in equal proportions, repeated at bed-time every second or third night."—Dr. Davis of Bristol Pauper Lunatic Asylum, "active purgatives with calomel"—Mr. Simpson of Grove Place, "a mild course of mercury"—Dr. Thurman at the Retreat, near York, "simple purgatives (with or without mercurial)" "a mild mercurial course, carried only to incipient ptyalism"—Dr. Mackinstosh of Newcastle-upon-Tyne Lunatic Asylum, "I have found opium in combination ith calomel soothing in acute mania."—Dr. Anderson of Haslar Hospital "Aperients of a mild character, such as small doses of calomel and colocynth"—Mr. Gillett of Fairwater Asylum, "Purgatives with calomel and tartar emetic"—Dr. Finch of Fisherton Asylum, "The protochloride of mercury in twelve grain doses, followed by croton oil, if they fail to have a purgative effect.", in the chronic stage, "mercury to affect the mouth"—Dr. Bucknill of Devon County Asylum, "the bowels open by one dose of calomel" "five or six grs. Of calomel is given when the state of the liver requires it"—Mr. Harris of Springfield Asylum, "mercury"—Drs. Miller and Shafter of St. Thomas's Hospital, "calomel on bread" where aperient medicines are refused—Dr. Sillery of the Military Lunatic Asylum at Yarmouth, in acute mania "free purgation with calomel and jalap"—Mr. Wilkes of Stafford County Lunatic Asylum, "a dose or two of calomel"—Dr. Palmer of Grove Hall, Bow, in the advanced stage, "five grains of mercury with chalk, and one-third, one-half, or two-thirds of a grain of morphia (hydrochlorate), every night", where there are paroxysms arising from epileptic irritation, a purgative of jalap and calomel, or of calomel with the common black draught, in dementia, decoction of cinchona with bichloride of mercury, purgatives preceded by calomel or gray powder

Remedies used in cases of Melancholia: Dr. Sutherland of St. Luke's Hospital, "in common melancholia, I have found pil. Hydrarg., or pil. Hyd. Chlor.c., continued for three or four months in some cases, do much good."—Mr. Casson of Hull and East Riding Asylum, where pulse is slow, "a small quantity of calomel, with opium, every night, followed in the morning by an aperient" where pulse is quick, blue pill and opiate at night—Mr. Poynder at

Kent County Lunatic Asylum, "mild mercurials"—Mr. Watson at Cumberland County Asylum "free purgation, by means of blue pill and colocynth"—Dr. Button of Dorset County, "mercurial alteratives"—Mr. Mallam of Hook Norton Asylum, "I frequently give one or more purgative doses of calomel,"—Dr. Oliver of Salop Asylum, "when the bowels are more obstinate, the compound extract of colocynth, with blue pill or calomel,"—Dr. Bryan of Horton House, "mercury as an alterative"—Dr. Anderson of the Lunatic Department of Haslar Hospital, calomel as an alterative—Dr. Finch of Fisherton Asylum, "large doses of calomel internally"—Dr. Bucknill of Devon County Asylum, "an occasional blue pill"—Mr. Wilkes, "alterative doses of calomel or blue pill when the functions of the liver is disordered"—Mr. Hill of Peckham House Asylum, "warm purgatives combined with mercurial"—Mr. Paul at Camberwell House, "small doses of blue pill"—Mr. Metcalfe, "pil. Hydrarg."

Remedies used in the Treatment of Epilepsy Dr. Sutherland of St. Lukes Hospital, where insanity follows epilepsy, bichloride of mercury of great use—Dr. Tyerman of the Cornwall County Asylum, calomel purgatives—Dr. Oliver of the Salop County Asylum, calomel—Dr. Davis of the Bristol Pauper Lunatic Asylum, mercury—Dr. Corsellis at the West York County Asylum, mercurial inunction—Dr. Gilliland at the Hereford Asylum, "a sharp purgative dose or two of calomel"—Dr. Finch of Fisherton House Asylum, "large doses of calomel"—Dr. Bucknill of Devon County Asylum "long continued use of mercurial alteratives"—Mr. Wilkes of Stafford County Asylum, "free exhibition of purgatives, as large doses of calomel and croton oil"

Remedies Used in Paralysis Dr. Sutherland of St. Lukes Hospital attributed two of the three cases of recovery from Paralysis to bichloride of mercury—Mr. Casson of Hull and East Riding Asylum, *"a* dose of calomel" and "alterative doses of mercury"—Dr, Button of Dorset County Lunatic Asylum, "mild mercurial course" in cases of paralysis—Dr, Tyerman of Cornwall County Asylum, "occasional mild aperients of calomel"—Dr. Bryan stated of Hoxton House, "mercury as an alterative is extremely serviceable" –Dr. Robinson Bensham Asylum, "the cautious employment of mercurials are frequently required"—Dr. Gilliland of Hereford Asylum, "mercurial purging"—Dr. Finch of Fisherton House Asylum, "mercury to affect the mouth"—Mr. Gaskell of Lancaster County Asylum, "the continued exhibition of small doses of bichloride of mercury"—Mr. Wilkes of Stafford County Asylum, "a mild mercurial course"—Dr. Connoly of Middlesex (or Hanwell) County Asylum, "small doses of calomel and squill have occasionally seemed useful."

Not every medicine used in the treatment of the insane was specifically called out. There were many, many instances in which asylum superintendents wrote merely that they found purgatives extremely useful, or that strict attention was paid to the state of the digestive organs or the bowels, practically catch phrases for the adjuvant or *supplemental* use of mercury.

By the 1870's, there was a growing appreciation that mercury might *cause* insanity, but where the tendency of angry irritability or violent excitement appeared to threaten a transition into mania, the lunacy doctors felt that "mercurials given to touch the gums, intermitted for six or eight weeks, and again given, ought, we think, to be tried. So many cases of this kind have recovered under this treatment, that, notwithstanding the contraindication of mercurial in Insanity, under the threatening circumstances above described, the patient ought not to be deprived of the chance thus afforded."[296] Unfortunately, Uncle Skeffington would

---

[296] Bucknill, J. Charles. (1879). *A manual of psychological medicine, containing the lunacy laws: the nosology, a ̃e ̃tiology, statistics, description, diagnosis,*

not be there to advise his nephew whether to take the chance afforded by mercury to stave off any impending madness. He was killed in 1873 by a blow to the head from a lunatic at one of the asylums he was visiting.

pathology, and treatment of insanity, with an appendix of cases. 4th ed. London: J. & A. Churchill, p 762.

Curiouser and Curiouser

I generally wrote down the answers, first of all, and afterwards the question and its solution.

-Lewis Carroll, Curiosa Mathematica

In 1888, just as Lewis Carroll was finishing up the first volume of his *Sylvie and Bruno* books, he published the first volume of his *Curiosa Mathematica,* titled, *A New Theory of Parallels.*[297] The book was published under Carroll's real name, Charles L. Dodgson, as were all of his mathematical works. Carroll did everything he could to maintain his privacy and to keep his identity as the author of *Alice* a secret. *A New Theory of Parallels* was reviewed in *Nature,* an apparently friendly review which nevertheless pointed out what the reviewer believed were faults in Dodgson's work. Dodgson immediately responded with a letter requesting that the reviewer reconsider some of the points he had made, and asking that the reviewer notify *Nature* readers that he was withdrawing his criticisms. Skillfully using Dodgson's own phrasing ("such an assumption would indeed be monstrous") against him, the reviewer printed an apology which was not one in fact.[298] A second edition was soon in the offing, in which Carroll replied in the preface to the criticisms, an event which prompted a reviewer from *The Athenaeum* to join the fray by objecting that that if Dodgson accepted Euclid's precepts, "he is bound to keep his assumptions within the boundaries which they prescribe. If he does not accept them, our objection, of course, falls to the

---

[297] Carroll, L. (1890). *Curiosa mathematica.* 3d ed. London: Macmillan.
[298] Lockyer, N. *Nature.*Vol 39, November 1888 to April 1889 [London and New York: Macmillan and Co., Mr. Dodgson on Parallels, Dec 6, 1888, pp 124-125, and Dec 20, 1888, p 175

ground; but in that case we must have strangely misunderstood the whole drift and purpose of the book." *That* comment was addressed by Dodgson in the preface to the 3rd edition, an increasingly unfriendly exchange which prompted the reviewer from *The Athenaeum* to question the spirit in which the reply was made, characterizing it as an unfair attack, despite the fact that it was apparently humourous ("he should strike fairly even when he strikes in fun"), and in return outing Dodgson as the author of *Alice* with a two faced barb, a striking example of subtle English insult, "We bear him no malice, however, and as a proof thereof we strongly recommend non mathematicians as well as mathematicians to read his witty and ingenious 'Curiosa,' which (if their experience agrees with ours) they will find as entertaining as little Alice found the curiosa of Wonderland."[299]

Readers would find it curious, in other words—bewildering and illogical.

The antagonized reviewer from *The Athenaeum* quickly dispatched Volume 2 of Carroll's *Curiosa Mathematica, Pillow Problems, thought out during Sleepless Nights* when it was published in 1893, stating that the introduction was much more interesting than the mathematical problems and solutions which followed, taking exception with the recommendation of mathematical exercises as a cure for insomnia, and stating that the last problem must be intended as a joke, containing, as it did, a fallacy in reasoning which might be easily exposed by a re-examination of elementary principles of probability.[300]

---

[299] *The Athenaeum*. 1889 July to December, London: John C. Francis, Science, No. 3232, Oct. 5.'89, p 457; 1891 July to December, London: John C. Francis, Curiosa Mathematica, No. 3328, Aug 8 '91, pp 196-197
[300] *The Athenaeum*. 1993 July to December, London: John C. Francis, Science, No. 3443, Oct. 21.'93

Nearly immediately, Carroll had a second edition issued in which the title was changed to *Pillow Problems, Thought Out During Wakeful Hours*, because Carroll did not like the apprehension the former title created in his readers (or reviewers) that he suffered from insomnia. He did not, he assured his readers in the preface to this later edition, it was merely that working out such problems in the head could prevent the entry of other unwanted worries of the day and help the reader sleep more easily, so that spending say, half an hour working out one of the problems, could prevent what might have been an hour wracked with *"harassing thoughts."* "The *real* dilemma, which I have had to face," he wrote, "is this: given that the brain is in so wakeful a condition that, do what I will, I am certain to remain awake for the next hour or so, I must choose between two courses, viz. either to submit to the fruitless self-torture of going through some worrying topic, over and over again, or else to dictate to myself some topic sufficiently absorbing to keep the worry at bay."[301] Of course, a restless wakeful state in which you can't let go of the thoughts in your head and fall asleep is the very definition of insomnia, so it is questionable whether Carroll achieved his goal in correcting that impression.

Addressing the possibility of errors, he wrote "My purpose—of giving this encouragement to others—would not be so well fulfilled had I allowed myself, in writing out my solutions, to improve on the work done in my head. I felt it to be much more important to set down what had actually been done in the head, than to supply shorter or neater solutions, which perhaps would be much harder to do without paper." The answers might not be

---

[301] Carroll, L. (1895). *Curiosa mathematica.* 4th ed. London: Macmillan and Co., preface to the Second edition 1893.

quite correct, he wrote, "but at least they are *genuine*, as the results of *mental* work *only."*

Previously, when we were discussing critics' statements that *Sylvie and Bruno* was incomprehensible, we entertained the possibility that Carroll was not seriously mentally deranged, but that he might be either out-thinking his audience, or being intentionally obscure in order to appear original. Now, thanks to Carroll's last problem of his 2nd Volume of *Curiosa Mathematica*, we have a clear cut illustration of something seriously wrong. Luckily, it does not depend on an understanding of Euclidian Geometry. For in this last attempt at mathematics by an Oxford University mathematics professor, Carroll has made such an obvious error that there isn't really any room for debate. He proudly offered the problem as one of the first in the field of "Transcendental Probabilities" and it was annotated with the date 8/9/87, which would have put its genesis squarely in the midst of Carroll's composition of the first *Sylvie and Bruno* books. The question read:

> *A bag contains 2 counters, as to which nothing is known except that each is either black or white. Ascertain their colours without taking them out of the bag.*
>
> *The answer given was simply: "One is black, the other white."*

Carroll warned that his answer might seem "abnormal or even paradoxical" to the casual reader. The correct answer, which has probably occurred to you, is that the counters might be, BB, BW, WB, or WW, or stated mathematically, there is a ¼ chance of that both counters are black, a ½ chance that one counter is black and one counter is white, and a ¼ chance that both counters are white. How could a mathematician and logician make such an elementary error? Luckily for us, Carroll explained his reasoning.

72. (18, 27)

We know that, if a bag contained 3 counters, 2 being black and one white, the chance of drawing a black one would be $\frac{2}{3}$; and that any *other* state of things would *not* give this chance.

Now the chances, that the given bag contains (a) *BB*, (β) *BW*, (γ) *WW*, are respectively $\frac{1}{4}$, $\frac{1}{2}$, $\frac{1}{4}$.

Add a black counter.

Then the chances, that it contains (a) *BBB*, (β) *BWB*, (γ) *WWB*, are, as before, $\frac{1}{4}$, $\frac{1}{2}$, $\frac{1}{4}$.

Hence the chance, of now drawing a black one,

$$= \tfrac{1}{4}\cdot 1 + \tfrac{1}{2}\cdot\tfrac{2}{3} + \tfrac{1}{4}\cdot\tfrac{1}{3} = \tfrac{2}{3}.$$

Hence the bag now contains *BBW* (since any *other* state of things would *not* give this chance).

Hence, before the black counter was added, it contained *BW*, i. e. one black counter and one white.

Q. E. F.

(Q. E. F. Quod erat faciendum—Latin for "which was to be done," a phrase used to demonstrate the proof of a geometric construction.)

The "Solution" which Carroll provided to prove his counter colour answer is incorrect. His *mathematics* are correct—it is his *assumptions* which are in error. Carroll's mistake was that he presumed the 2/3 *chance* of drawing a black counter to be the same thing as a *physical/real* situation in which 2 out of 3 counters were black (BBW), and worked *backwards* from it to achieve his answer (BW), which follows naturally from his first assumption (BBW – B = BW), but this situation does not yield the same probabilities as if you had placed 1 black counter in a bag with 2 *random* counters. Carroll's black and white counter problem was almost certainly suggested by Augustus De Morgan's essay on determining inverse probabilities in the case of an unknown mix of black and white balls.[302] Carroll modeled so many of his problems on those of De Morgan that it was likely the men came to know each other. In this spirit, consider the statement made by De Morgan that a mathematician friend of his "whom I must not name", had conceived up to 800 anagrams of De Morgan's name "during some sleepless nights."[303]

In his younger years, Carroll had excelled at spooling out subtle chains of logic which forced the listener to reach a false or absurd conclusion. It was the magic which underlay his best works. Ironically, Carroll set himself up to make his own error in logic—and perhaps it was because he worked the problem out while in a dream state. Carroll made a point of remarking that nearly all of the problems presented had the same history, they had begun as interesting ideas which Carroll had worked out mentally before going to sleep, the answers to which had occurred to him upon waking. It was the same form of subconscious inspiration that he had been using more and more within his fiction, used now for his mathematics as well. Later reviewers would choose this period in Carroll's life to say that it was at this point Lewis Carroll had died.

> When "Sylvie and Bruno Concluded" was written, Lewis Carroll had died. He who had brought the world to his reduction ad absurdum had descended into the dull Charles Dodgson.[304]

It's an unfair statement, to parse the man out like that, and say, the one we liked is gone, and the one we never liked is all

---

[302] Morgan, A. (1838). *An essay on probabilities: and their application to life contingencies and insurance offices.* London: Longman, Orme, Brown, Green & Longmans, pp 53-68.

[303] De Morgan, A. (1872). *A budget of paradoxes.* London: Longmans, Green, and Co., pp 82-83.

[304] Carroll, L. (1936). *The Lewis Carroll book.* New York: Dial Press., xvi, preface by Richard Herrick

that is left over, because the truth is, that at this point, Charles Dodgson was lost as well. In 1878 Dodgson had begun to become increasingly withdrawn and antisocial. He stopped giving the dinner parties he had been so found of, and he instituted a policy of refusing all social invitations. In 1880 he gave up his "one amusement," photography, and in 1881 he gave up his mathematical lectureship. In 1882 he was afflicted with some kind of skin disorder, an oval patch of pink shining skin under one arm. It wasn't serious, but he doubted his homeopath's diagnosis of tinnea, and it was at this point that he began to turn to traditional doctors and their medicines. He was increasingly afflicted with ague, a recurring intermittent fever, and he began to be troubled by lameness and pain in his knees. *Was* Lewis Carroll prescribed mercury for his many complaints?

Mercury was used as a specific treatment of *every* illness which Lewis Carroll experienced, in eye complaints, and tinnea, in vesicle catarrh and cystitis, in the intermittent fever known as ague, in inflammation of the knee's synovial membrane due both to injury and to constitutional issues such as rheumatism, for migraine headaches and epileptiform convulsions, in acute laryngitis and pneumonia, and when one's mind was slipping. And the most incriminating, saddening thing of all is that, with the exception of ague, which was caused by malarial microorganisms, mercury was not only used in treatment, but was also capable of *causing* each and every one of these complaints..

The problem with his knees was especially troubling to Carroll as it prevented him from taking the long nature walks that he so loved. First it was the left knee which pained him, but then the pain moved to his right knee. In March of 1890, it returned in the left, suggesting, as Carroll wrote, a systemic "probably rheumatic" cause of the distress. He began to experience serious back pain around the same time. He was in the midst of writing *Sylvie and*

Bruno Concluded, and he made his Professor character suffer "lumbago and rheumatism, and that kind of thing" as well. The Professor, at least, had been "curing himself" with his advanced knowledge of medicine.[305] We don't know if Carroll resorted to any kind of self-help himself, but we do know, that like the Professor, Carroll "was a reader of medical books, knew his 'bones', and had a good layman's knowledge of medical facts."[306]

Mercurial ointments and blue pill had been used for the inflammation of the knee's synovial membrane for at least 100 years, beginning before Lewis Carroll was born, and continuing after his death. This was the case even more so when the inflammation would subside in one joint, only to re-appear in another, an occurrence which tended to indicate that its cause was due, not to injury, but to a constitutional disease.[307] In January of 1892 Carroll would write that his knee was not better, and that he was living as a hermit. Again and again he would write that he was a prisoner, that he was laid up, that he had stayed in due to his recurring knee and back pain. When Carroll

---

[305] Carroll, L. (1889). *Sylvie and Bruno*. London: Macmillan, p 11.

[306] Elton, O. (1906). *Frederick York Powell: a life and a selection from his letters and occasional writings.* Oxford: The Clarendon press. , p 362

[307] *Further Observations on the Diseases which affect the **Synovial** Membranes of Joints*, B. C. Brodie, Med Chir Trans. 1814; 5: 239–254. ("Inflammation of the synovial membranes may occur as a symptom of a constitutional disease, where the system is affected by rheumatism, where mercury has been exhibited Improperly, or inlarge quantities, or where there is general debility from any other cause."); Oleate of mercury good for persistant inflammation of joints, including synovitis Ringer, S. (1878). *A handbook of therapeutics.* London: H.K. Lewis. Pp 226-227 (underlying paper quoted, John Marshall); Barwell, R. (1881). *A treatise on diseases of the joints.* 2d ed., rev. & much enl. New York: W. Wood & co., p154 (blue pill as part of the treatment for synovitis); Phillips, C. D. F. 1830-1904. (1882). *Materia medica & therapeutics: inorganic substances.* London: J.& A. Churchill, p 653 (Scotts mercurial ointment on strips with strapping for chronic synovitis.); *A Case of Symmetrical **Synovitis** of Knees*, W. Rowley Bristow, Proc R Soc Med. 1926; 19(Sect Orthop): 31–32 (Little girl's synovitis treated with mercurial inunctions.)

had been practicing homeopathic medicine he had been quite specific in his diary about the things he was using to treat himself, but now that he was seeing traditional doctors, and plenty of them, his entries regarding the therapies prescribed were vague, as, for example, this May 1893 entry "After a week indoors, taking Dr. Brooks' medicine to set the liver etc. right, I have returned to my ordinary ways."[308]

Not only was Carroll's knee and back pain keeping him in and making him feel like a hermit, but his increasing lack of social contact was making him feel like a recluse. Nevertheless, he maintained his refusal to accept social invitations quite strictly, writing in March of 1884 that he had been declining all invitations for the past *six years*, and when he was forced into a party he could not escape, he would write in his diary later that the small talk had been an effort, that it was tiring, and depressing. An acquaintance would describe him later as having "an unreadiness in conversation."[309] It is a description which socially anxious readers will recognize as a perfect description of a complex and practically indescribable inhibition.

In February of 1894, Carroll wrote,

As Ragg was reading Prayers, and Bayne and I were the only M.A.'s in the stalls, I tried the experiment of going to the lectern and reading the lesson. I did not hesitate much, but feel it too great a strain on the nerves to be tried often.[310]

---

[308] Wakeling, E. (2001) Lewis Carroll's Diaries, The Private Journals of Charles Lutwidge Dodgson, Vol 9, p 65

[309] Traill, H. D. 1842-1900., Birrell, A. (1898). *Among my books: papers on literary subjects by the following writers Augustine Birrell ... [and 18 others] reprinted from 'Literature' ; with a preface by H.D. Traill.* London: Elliot Stock., p 110

[310] Collingwood, S. Dodgson. (1899). *The life and letters of Lewis Carroll (Rev. C.L. Dodgson).* New York: The Century Co. p 333

It was quite a contrast to the young man who had kept his friends laughing with his quick wit, and who, despite his problems with hesitation of speech, had been able to perform sermons on short notice before large congregations. In June of 1894, *sixteen years* after deciding to decline all social invitations, he wrote to Mrs. Paget, who he knew well, declining an invitation to breakfast, and begging to be excused on the grounds that "to accept one such invitation would put me in a false position as to all others."[311] On December 23, 1897, the 65 year old Lewis Carroll traveled to Guildford to spend Christmas with his sisters. His nephew would later write, "He seemed to be in his ordinary health, and in the best of spirits, and there was nothing to show that the end was so near." He must have been in somewhat *better* health and spirits than he had been in recent years as he had spent more than one Christmas alone at Oxford, afraid to travel lest he have a convulsive fit en route. Once at Guildford he spent his time hard at work on the second part of his planned three part Symbolic Logic series. Carroll had published *Elementary Symbolic Logic* in 1896, and he planned on publishing the next two books, *Advanced* and *Transcendental Symbolic Logic* within the next few years.[312] He fell sick shortly after the New Year, however, with a slight hoarseness which made speaking difficult. "At first his illness seemed a trifle," wrote his nephew, "but before a week had passed bronchial symptoms had developed, and Dr. Gabb, the family physician, ordered him to keep to his bed. His breathing rapidly became hard and laborious." He fell into a delirium and died soon after, on January the 14th.[313]

---

[311] Wakeling, E. (2001) Lewis Carroll's Diaries, The Private Journals of Charles Lutwidge Dodgson, Vol 9, p 152.

[312] Carroll, L. (1896). *Symbolic logic: part I, elementary.* London: Macmillan.

[313] Collingwood, S. Dodgson. (1899). *The life and letters of Lewis Carroll (Rev.*

Of Dr. J. P. A. Gabb who was called in to oversee Lewis Carroll's care, not much is known. He had received his M.D. with honours, and had been in practice in Guildford for 15 years at the time he oversaw Carroll's last illness. He was a shy man with a good sense of humour, and he was dedicated to his patients.[314] He had risked his life once to save a young boy from drowning.[315] What had the heroic Dr. Gabb done to try to save the famous Lewis Carroll?

Mercury was often employed for throat affectations, including pain on swallowing, inflammatory swelling, and membranous croup.[316] Because doctors saw many cases of sore throats preceding intense general infection and death within a few days, calomel was often employed early in the case of a sore throat on the *chance* that the sore throat might be the first indication of a deadly bacterial illness, such as the upper respiratory tract illness diphtheria. In 1897 the British Medical Journal published an American Physician's statement advocating calomel in the case of *all* sore-throats, "Believing, as I do, that all sore-throats, where the tonsils are involved and where false membrane exists, are in some degree related to diphtheria, I never hesitate to exhibit calomel in small doses at first, and by its action prove or disprove the diptheritic tendency of the case."[317] Calomel was making a strong resurgence at the end of the 1800s, and a brisk calomel purge was often employed at the outset of pneumonia and other respiratory complaints.[318] In the latter half of 1897, *The*

C.L. Dodgson). New York: The Century Co. pp 346-348

[314] Obituary, J.P.A. Gabb, M.D., Br Med J. Oct 13, 1934; 2(3849): 702.

[315] (1862). *The Quiver: an illustrated magazine for Sunday and general reading.* Vol 23 (1888) London: Cassell and Co., Ltd., p. 72

[316] Hahnemann, S. (1894). *Hahnemann's therapeutic hints.* London: E. Gould & Son, p. 24-25. 41

[317] British Medical Journal 1897 Judd, p 210; Leonardo D. Judd, Calomel as a Curative Agent in Diphtheria, Trans Am Climatol Assoc. 1897; 13: 206–213.

Practitioner reported that the German doctor G. Freudenthal was recommending calomel as a means of aborting influenza ("two or three large doses of calomel are given on the onset of the symptoms"[319]), and even as much as 15 years later doctors were still using calomel in pneumonia, as evidenced by the following report:

> "Directly pneumonia has been diagnosed, I commence by giving 4 grains of calomel, which is continued in doses of 2 to 4 grains every day or every second day, according to the state of the bowels, till the temperature falls. In every instance the most noticeable favourable sign is the patient is able to get some sleep. Equally beneficial effect is seen in ulcerative tonsillitis with thick white membrane deposit or sloughy base, which may be said to clear up in double quick time. Of course, calomel in either case is used as a routine adjuvant and not as a specific. What I mean is, calomel lavage is looked upon as an essential part of the treatment with appropriate remedies, and not relied upon per se."[320]

What happened during that second week of January in 1898 at the Dodgson home in Guildford? We cannot know. The past conceals the events which have taken place within it, as a river conceals those things which have settled to the bottom of its bed. If the river is shallow, you might be able to see what lies beneath, if the time passed is not long, you might be able to find people still alive who can point to the shapes within and recall their form. Shortly after Lewis Carroll died and his biographers were

---

[318] *The Practitioner.* Vol. 71 (1903) London: *John* Brigg, p 888; Clinical Lectures on Pneumonia, Delivered at the Liverpool Royal Infirmary, March, 1900, James Barr, Br Med J. 1900 June 16; 1(2059): 1461–1467
[319]*The Practitioner.* Old Series, Vol LIX, New Series Vol. VI July to December 1897, London: Cassell and Company, Limited, p. 553
[320] The Treatment of Pneumonia, D. N. Cooper, Br Med J. 1913 August 23; 2(2747): 522.

gathering all the information they could about his life, they did not understand the implications of the great amount of mercury that had been given to the generation passing away. They were unaware, also, of the hatter/mercury connection which might have led them to ask the right questions about mercury use in Carroll's own life while there was still time to find the truth. It was not until the second and third decades of the 1900's that in-depth investigations began to be published on the *emotional effects* of the use of mercury in industry, and the term mad as a hatter began to be understood more widely for the mercury poisoning it referred to, and people began to understand why it was *hatters* who were mad, and not shoemakers, or tailors. Long after Lewis Carroll had died.

An After Thought

A year ago I was browsing online videos to view those which dealt with the emotional symptoms of mercury poisoning. There were several quite good ones, including one put together as a presentation for a neurology class which specifically discussed the Mad Hatter. I thought it very silly to discuss whether a literary character might or might not have mercury poisoning, and commented accordingly, which only goes to show how liable we all are to plot out our own little areas of interest and to disregard what lies outside those boundaries. I was soon convinced by the replies I received to my comment that whether the Mad Hatter was intended to have mercury poisoning *mattered*, and I set out to research the issue.

I wasn't a Lewis Carroll scholar, or a Carrollian, as they call themselves, but a *mercury* scholar, for which there is as yet no name which doesn't have negative connotations of fanaticism and lack of perspective. But as someone who has researched the history of mercury use extensively, I knew just how widespread its use was during the course of Lewis Carroll's lifetime, and I believed that if I could find evidence of mercury use by Carroll, it might be fairly easy to prove that the Hatter was intended to be similarly affected. A quick first look convinced me that there might be something there to be found—the Hatter was easy and silly in non-threatening company, but stammering and nervous under pressure, and Carroll, similarly, was described as stammering and having the sort of nervousness which is intensified in the presence of strangers. I didn't expect to find such clear evidence that the Hatter was *not* intended to be suffering from mercury poisoning, except that which unintentionally present in the Hatter's role as Carroll's doppelganger. I also did not expect to be so frustratingly unable to find definitive evidence of mercury use by Carroll *beyond that involved in his* photography. It wasn't for lack of trying. Knowing that the Carrollians would have been unlikely to have overlooked mercury use recorded by Carroll, I gathered the names of all Carroll's doctors and searched for case notes, not of Carroll's case, but of others, to try to prove a pattern of prescription and use, but there is so little left of those men. Carroll's homeopath Schuldman did recommend mercurial medications for clergyman's sore throat, but those were homeopathic medicines, and any mercury in them would have been diluted to the point of absolute harmlessness. One of the men who treated Carroll's synovitis used mercurial washes as an antiseptic in knee surgery, but Carroll did not have knee surgery. In the end, I would have to say there is absence of *direct* evidence of medicinal mercury use in Carroll's life, but absence of evidence is not evidence of absence. I believe that, in light of the overwhelming prevalence of mercurial medications in Carroll's lifetime, and in light of the characteristic pattern of his physical and mental decay, it is *overwhelmingly likely* that he also took such medications. Whether I have proved that or not to *your* satisfaction is another matter, but in the end, what I would most like to accomplish with this book is to raise the issue as one of legitimate discussion. When Carroll introduced his one problem on "transcendental probabilities", he used quotation marks around the term, just as I have to indicate it as a term used previously be another, and a search of the earlier literature using that term has revealed the likely source, an 1878 book titled *A Candid Examination of Theism* by a man who identified himself simply as Physicus.[321] Physicus'

---

[321] Romanes, G. John. (1878). *A candid examination of theism.* 3d ed. London: K. Paul, Trench, Trübner, & co.., p 66

book was an attempt to use logic to prove the existence of God, and there is no doubt that Carroll, as a logician *and* a clergyman, would have been most interested in it. And what is more, Carroll knew Physicus, whose real name was George John Romanes. Carroll had personally signed Romanes' name into the Christ Church Common Room book when Romanes became a member of Christ Church, Oxford, in the summer of 1890.[322]

In his book, Romanes/Physicus said, "men find conceivability a valid test of truth in the affairs of everyday life, its validity decreasing in proportion to the distance at which the test is applied from the sphere of experience."[323] It is my hope that the world I have uncovered for you has made these theories *conceivable* to you, despite the fact that its evidence lies so far in the past, because what is a theory to us was a life for the man, and it deserves to be known. The past conceals two facts, both of which are either true or false—a transcendental probability, unknowable. For you to ascertain.

---

[322] Romanes, G. John. (1896). *The life and letters of George John Romanes.* [2d ed.] London: Longmans, Green., pp 257-258

[323] Physicus (1878). *A candid examination of theism.* 3d ed. London: K. Paul, Trench, Trübner, & co.. P 19

Made in the USA
Lexington, KY
19 December 2018